Exeter Medieval English Texts and Studies

General Editors: Marion Glasscoe and M. J. Swanton

The Vercelli Book f. 133

CYNEWULF'S
'ELENE'

Edited by

P. O. E. GRADON

UNIVERSITY OF EXETER PRESS

First published in Methuen's Old English Library in 1958

Revised edition, University of Exeter Press 1977
Reprinted 1980, 1992

This revised edition published in 1996 by
University of Exeter Press
Reed Hall, Streatham Drive
Exeter, Devon EX4 4QR
UK

ISBN 0 85989 508 4

Printed and bound by CPI Group (UK) Ltd, Croydon, CR0 4YY

PREFACE

THE aim of this edition has been to sift the mass of criticism, emendation and speculation which has grown up round the text. In order to bring the work into conformity with the requirements of the series in which it is published it has been necessary in view of the length of the text to reduce the apparatus to a minimum; but it is hoped that the bibliography will afford sufficient guidance to the considerable literature on the text.

The editor has pleasure in acknowledging the help received from the Bodleian Library and the Cambridge University Library; to whose courtesy she is indebted for photostats of Marsh 13 and MS Mm. 6. 4 respectively. She also wishes to thank the Prefect of the Vatican Library for providing photostats of Vatican MS Graec. 2048 and the Librarian of the St Gall Stiftsbibliothek for photostats of St Gall MS 225. To the authorities of the British Museum she owes thanks for their invariable courtesy and in particular to Dr Cyril Moss of the department of Oriental Printed Books and Manuscripts for his very generous help in checking the collation of the Syriac versions of the *Inventio Crucis* from the originals.

The editor's thanks are also due to Canonico Marinone, Archivist of the Eusebian Archives at Vercelli, for enabling her to collate the manuscript, to the Worshipful Masters of the Bench for permission to consult Maier's transcript and the correspondence of Charles Purton Cooper in the Library at Lincoln's Inn, and to the Deputy Keeper of the Records for permission to consult the records of the issue of the Appendices of Cooper's Report on Rymer's *Foedera*. The research in which the book originated was aided by a grant from the Central Research Fund of the University of London, which enabled her to visit Vercelli to see the manuscript.

Dr Kenneth Brooks and Mr Neil Ker have contributed materially to the work; the former by the loan of his manuscript edition of *Andreas* and by many helpful suggestions; the latter by drawing the editor's attention to the presence at

Lincoln's Inn of Maier's transcript. Unfortunately Mr Ker's *Catalogue of MSS containing Anglo-Saxon*, to which the editor is also indebted, came to hand too late to be included in the bibliography. The set of Ἐκκλησιαστικὴ Ἀλήθεια used in the discussion of the source she owes to the kindness of Canon J. A. Douglas to whom it belongs. Finally the editor wishes to thank Professor C. L. Wrenn for the interest sustained since the work's inception in 1944.

OXFORD
1956

PREFACE TO THE REVISED EDITION

For this revised edition the Bibliography has been supplemented to take account of the continuing work on the poem and its background.

M. J. SWANTON, EXETER
1996

CONTENTS

ABBREVIATIONS

AEW	F. Holthausen, *Altenglisches Etymologisches Wörterbuch*
AfdA	*Anzeiger für deutsches Alterthum*
Anglia Beibl . . ˙.	*Anglia Beiblatt*
Archiv	*(Herrigs) Archiv für das Studium der neueren Sprachen u. Literaturen*
BB	*Bonner Beiträge zur Anglistik*
BT, BTS	J. Bosworth and T. N. Toller, *An Anglo-Saxon Dictionary* and Supplement
Bülbring	K. D. Bülbring, *Altenglisches Elementarbuch*
BZ	*Byzantinische Zeitschrift*
EETS	Early English Text Society
EPNS	Publications of the English Place Name Society
ESt	*Englische Studien*
Gött. gel. Anz. . .	*Göttingische gelehrte Anzeigen*
Grein-Köhler . . .	C. W. M. Grein, *Sprachschatz der ags. Dichter* revised G. Köhler
HBS	Henry Bradshaw Society
JEGPh	*Journal of English and Germanic Philology*
JJJ	E. A. Kock, *Jubilee Jaunts and Jottings*, Lunds Universitets Aarskrift, N.F. Pt. i, Vol. xiv (2)
Lindisf.	Lindisfarne Gospels
MGH	*Monumenta Germaniae Historica*, ed. G. Pertz
MLA	Publications of the Modern Language Association of America
MLN	*Modern Language Notes*
MLR	*Modern Language Review*
MPh	*Modern Philology*
NED	*New English Dictionary*
PBB	*Beiträge zur Geschichte der deutschen Sprache un- ˙ Literatur*, ed. H. Paul and W. Braune
PL	*Patrologiae cursus completus;* series latina, ed. J. P. Migne

ix

CYNEWULF'S ELENE

INTRODUCTION

I. HISTORY AND DESCRIPTION OF THE TEXT

THE manuscript of *Elene*, the Vercelli Book, is now No. CXVII in the Eusebian Archives at Vercelli in northern Italy.[1] The manuscript consists of 136 leaves of thin parchment each of which has from 23 to 33 lines of writing. The last folio has been left blank while others, in each case the concluding folio of an item, are only partly filled. Each leaf is about 20 by 31 centimetres in size. Ruled lines and margins appear on both recto and verso folios. *Elene* follows Homily xxii and extends from f. 121 to f. 133[b]. *Elene* and the following homily on St Guthlac together form the eighteenth and nineteenth gatherings of the manuscript, the eighteenth gathering extending from f. 121 to f. 128 and the nineteenth from f. 129 to f. 135. The last leaf has been attached to the back of gathering XIX. These gatherings have been marked and numbered, probably in a later hand, by placing at the head of the first page of each a roman numeral, and at the foot of the last page of each one of the letters of the alphabet from A to T. Damage to the manuscript seems to have obliterated the letter T at the end of gathering XIX, but the letter S is visible on f. 128[b] and the numerals xviii and xix on ff. 121, 129.

There are numerous tears and holes. Small holes appear in the text of *Elene* on f. 131[b] above *hrusan* 1091; on f. 131 above the *s* of *piðsóc* 1039 and in many other instances. These sometimes damage a letter in the text although in no case do they affect legibility. Such holes appear on f. 122 in the *e* of *róde* 103; on 124[b] in the first *ȝ* of *ȝinȝne* 353; on f. 127[b] in the *e* of *piðsæcest* 663 and so on. But the reagent, used with such disastrous results in some parts of the manuscript, has not affected the text of *Elene*.[2] The large oval stain after *fór* on

---

[1] For accounts of the manuscript see p. 76.

[2] Cp f. 54[a]. Examination of the manuscript shows that the stain which appears to cover part of *Fates* 96–122 has destroyed the writing. Only the writing on the other side can now be seen. The letters *Pa?*, read by Maier in line 100, appear to be the *ær* of *mæran* on the other side.

I

f. 121 just covers, but does not obscure, the final stroke of the *r*. But many pages show discoloration and smudging. Folio 125, in particular, is stained and blotted although the text is legible. The parchment on f. 125ᵇ is badly discoloured. The numerous tears and holes in the margins, many of them repaired by the Vatican in 1913, do not affect the text's legibility.

The handwriting is a tenth-century Anglo-Irish hand from the south of England. Keller supposed the manuscript to have been written between 960 and 980. Förster, on the other hand, thinks it impossible to date so precisely, since the character of handwriting depends partly on the scribe's age and the conventions of his scriptorium. In the Vercelli Book, the comparative accuracy and regularity of the script suggest an experienced scribe and Förster, therefore, dates rather less precisely than Keller in the second half of the tenth century.[1] As evidence of a date at the beginning of this period he notes that Latin words are written in insular script and not, as became usual towards the end of the tenth century, in Frankish cursive. There are no grounds for assuming that the manuscript is in more than one hand although the writing becomes noticeably smaller on f. 131ᵇ after *ʒodʒimmas*.[2]

The manuscript is plain in appearance although ornamental capitals introduce homilies xix and xxi and line 1478 of *Andreas*. These have been shown by Wormald to derive from types found in MS Junius 27.[3] On ff. 47ᵇ and 51 the roundels of the capitals are filled or partly filled with a scallop pattern thought by Förster to be reminiscent of Irish work. One or more plain capitals introduce each homily and each lection of the poems. Only in *Elene* are the lections numbered. The cover, which dates from the nineteenth century, is of tooled leather and has on the spine in black letters: *Homiliarum Liber ignoti idiomatis* | 41 | Secolo x | cxvii.

---

[1] See Keller, *Palaestra* xliii. 33, 39–40; Förster, *Codice Vercellese* 11–14.

[2] Cp Wülcker, *Codex Vercellensis* vii; Napier, ZfdA xxxiii. 67. Later additions are noted in the textual variants. For marginal additions see Krapp, *Vercelli Book* xv–xvi; Sisam, *Studies in the History of Old English Literature* 109–18.

[3] *Archaeologia* xci. 120, 134.

History of the Text

The origin of the Vercelli Book is unknown. The language of the codex contributes little to a solution of the problem, since few features are common to the whole.[1] The spelling -*et* for -*eþ* in verbal forms is Anglian and Kentish, but its occurrence is sporadic.[2] Forms such as *ʒionlic, camwerod, camrædenne, ʒeonsiðe* (MS. ʒeon, on siðe), *lansceare, ʒirsandæʒ* may be Kentish since comparable forms occur, for instance, in the Kentish gloss in Vespasian D vi, the Canterbury Psalter and Textus Roffensis. But comparable forms occur in late West Saxon texts also.[3] The most common features of the manuscript spelling are the diphthong *io* and the doubling and shortening of consonants. The latter is late Old English, the former Kentish or early West Saxon, but such spellings are more frequent in the homilies than in the poems. They could be due to the use of a Kentish or West Saxon homiliary for part of the collection. But in view of the sprinkling of probably Kentish forms they may rather represent the lapses of a Kentishman writing the West Saxon *koine*.[4] Briefly, the language of the manuscript is at best an equivocal witness. More suggestive are the parallels between the Vercelli Book and the Exeter Book, which in view of its resemblance to MS Lambeth 149, is held to be of western provenance.[5] But the significance of these parallels is also

[1] Förster believed that the language indicated a connection with St Mary's, Worcester, and he refers to striking similarities between the language of the Vercelli Book and Wulfgeat's manuscripts of Wulfstan's homilies. But the dialect blend noted by Dunkhase can be otherwise explained.

[2] See f. 62 4; f. 110 20; *Soul and Body* 105, 132. Cp Sievers-Brunner § 357 n3. But cp Schlemilch, *Sprachdenkmäler der Übergangszeit* 56–7.

[3] f. 62 20, f. 83ᵇ 14; f. 112ᵇ 12; *Andreas*, 4, 501; f. 73ᵇ 17. Brotanek, Anglia Beibl xxvi. 235. Cp Luick § 677.

[4] Cp Sisam, *Studies* 153. The unrounding of *y* (which is primarily although not quite exclusively Kentish) occurs in *wyrðmendo* f. 89ᵇ 24; *wyrðment* f. 116 30–1; *ʒefellan* f. 16 15; *ʒeðeldelice* f. 5ᵇ 17; *ʒerene* f. 88 20; cp *acynned = acenned* f. 86ᵇ 13. Possibly Kentish is the peculiar spelling *dieorwyrðum* f. 70 6 but most probably it represents an attempted correction of *io* to *eo*.

[5] A miscellany somewhat parallel in content to the Exeter Book is mentioned in a medieval catalogue from Glastonbury: *Vita Sancti*

ambiguous. Thus both have the *Soul and Body* poem, but the appearance of *Azarias* in both the Exeter Book and the Cædmon Manuscript warns against the easy assumption that similarity of content proves identity of origin; both manuscripts have signed poems of Cynewulf; but a common place of origin for the two manuscripts presupposes a shared manuscript or manuscripts of Cynewulf's poetry. The choice of two Cynewulfian poems apiece for each codex might then be thought strangely arbitrary. There are the curious parallels between Vercelli homily x and *The Wanderer* but these may be due to the use of a common source. Both the Vercelli Book and the Exeter Book have lives of St Guthlac, but the cult of the saint had probably spread beyond Mercia by the tenth century. This is implied by the varied provenance of the manuscripts of Felix of Crowland's Life (notably C.C.C.C. 389, a Canterbury book); by the frequent appearance of his festival in ecclesiastical calendars [1] of varied provenance; by the existence of a proper mass for the saint in the Missal of Robert of Jumièges, thought by the Henry Bradshaw Society editor to be a Winchester book but possibly South-Western in origin.[2] His cult may have spread from a western centre such as Glastonbury, Worcester or Hereford [3] and was perhaps partly due to an association between the austerity of the eremitical life and the new monasticism.[4]

Gutlaci et liber Pronosticorum & de animabus defunctorum & de ultima resurrexione et aenigmata multorum (John of Glastonbury's Chronicle, ed. Hearne 436).

[1] See Wormald, *English Calendars before 1100* (HBS lxxii) esp. nos. 3, 5–7, 10–14, 16, 17. These entries, although no doubt in part martyrological only, contrast strongly with the very limited incidence of, for example, St Pega, who amongst the calendars cited, appears only in Douce 296 and Lambeth 873 probably both Crowland books (cp N. R. Ker, *Medieval Libraries of Great Britain*). She appears in the probably Mercian Martyrology. (Cp Felix' *Life of Guthlac* ed. Colgrave (9–10) which was not available before this book went to press.)

[2] Ed. Wilson (HBS xi). Cp Sisam, *Studies* 9. A proper mass for the saint appears also in Vitellius A xviii (Warren, Leofric Missal 303–4).

[3] Offices for the saint appear in the 13 c. Hereford Breviary (HBS xl) and fragments in C.C.C.C. 198, a Worcester book (cp N. R. Ker, *op. cit.*).   [4] Cp Bishop, *The Bosworth Psalter* 23.

4

There seems therefore no cogent reason for associating the Vercelli Book with the west. The Glastonbury Calendar indeed which seems to have been the basis of both the calendar in the Leofric Missal and the calendar in the Bosworth Psalter,[1] a Canterbury book, may well serve to remind us that ecclesiastical as well as linguistic affinities are significant for manuscript origins. Perhaps further research on the origin of the Vercelli Book might usefully start from the hypothesis that it is a Winchester or Canterbury book (perhaps with Glastonbury antecedents) rather than a Worcester one as Förster thought.[2]

The Vercelli Codex may have been given its present form by the scribe. The collection does not follow the church calendar but is a series of penitential homilies covering mainly the traditional themes of meditation: *Mors tua, mors domini, nota culpe, gaudia celi*. That the collection is composite may be suggested by the appearance of the numbers ii, iii, iiii, v, vi preceding homilies VII–XI. Had this numbering represented merely the numbering of the homilies in relation to the Fates of the Apostles we might have expected the number i before homily VI which immediately follows the Fates of the Apostles.[3] Instead the number xvi heads this homily representing possibly an old quire signature. The apparent lack of a number i in that case is, perhaps, due to its having appeared at the end of the concluding item of quire xv of the exemplar.[4]

[1] See Bishop, *The Bosworth Psalter*.

[2] It is interesting to notice that the sign *xɓ* which appears in the Vercelli Book is common in Canterbury manuscripts. Cp Sisam, *Studies* 109–10. The resemblance between the capital on f. 49 of the Vercelli Book and the capitals in the Junius Manuscript is also suggestive but Wormald has pointed out that this style is 'part of the common vocabulary of English illuminators of that time', *Archaeologia* xci. 119.

[3] But it is perhaps to be seen at the bottom of f. 54ᵇ. Cp Ker, *Catalogue of MSS*, p. 461.

[4] Another possible indication of mechanical copying appears on f. 109ᵇ where the scribe has left a blank for a capital which has in fact been supplied. The use of superscriptions and capitalization at the beginning of the items is haphazard by comparison with such a manuscript as, for example, Bodley 340/342 and may perhaps represent different scribal traditions, thus indicating the different components of the manuscript. For linguistic evidence see Peterson, *Studies in Philology* l. 559–65.

The collection cannot have been completed much before the middle of the ninth century since the eleventh homily refers to the Danish invasions. The use of apocryphal material in the fifteenth and twenty-second homilies suggests a tenth-century date, for the Blickling Homilies, the Homilies attributed to Wulfstan, and Ælfric's preface to the Catholic Homilies all witness an interest in apocryphal literature after about 900. Förster, moreover, calls attention to references to the end of the world in homilies xi and xv. Some of the prose material in the codex may, thus, date from the ninth or tenth century, but more probably from the tenth, while the whole codex may represent either the autograph of the collector or an apograph.

How the manuscript came to Vercelli is not known. Dr Sisam, however, has shown that the fragment of a psalm with neums on f. 24^b suggests that the manuscript was at Vercelli already in the eleventh century although it was still in England when a hand later than the scribe's wrote *writ thus* on f. 63b, *sclean* on f. 99 and scribbles on the last folio.[1] It is thus possible to discount both the view of Neigebaur that the manuscript was taken to Vercelli at the time of the Renaissance and the Cardinal Guala theory first put forward in 1844. Whether Vercelli in fact possessed a hostel for English pilgrims as Wülcker thought, or whether the manuscript was taken to Vercelli by Bishop Ulf of Dorchester, may be doubted; but, since Vercelli was on the main pilgrim route to Rome, the possibilities are evidently numerous.

The first certain reference to the codex is in a letter written in 1748 from the bibliophile, Giuseppe Bianchini of Verona, to Cardinal Vittorio delle Lancie. In this letter he not only describes the manuscript but transcribes a passage, which, for all its errors, is clearly taken from ff. 85^b–86 of the Vercelli Book.[2] Bianchini's discovery, however, attracted little attention and

---

[1] Sisam, *Studies* 109–18.
[2] See G. de-Gregory, *Istoria della Vercellese Letteratura ed Arti* iv. 554–60. Förster also draws attention to the entry *Liber Gothicus sive Longobardus* in an inventory of 1602. This book, although numbered XC, may have been the Vercelli Book.

6

the manuscript became widely known only after its rediscovery in the early nineteenth century.

In the years 1821–3, the jurist Friedrich Blume made a tour of Italian libraries to collect material for his study of roman law. Between October 27 and November 19 of 1822 he examined the chapter library at Vercelli where, among other manuscripts, he inspected the Vercelli Book, which he says contains 'Legenden oder Homilien in "angelsäxischer Sprache" '.[1] The news of the discovery soon spread in England and Germany. Blume spoke of it to the German antiquary Lappenberg who, on September 18 1832, wrote to Charles Purton Cooper telling him of Blume's discovery and referring him to a forthcoming description of it in the *Rheinisches Museum* by Jacob Grimm.[2] Negotiations followed with a view to borrowing the manuscript or making a copy [3] and Cooper having obtained a specimen of the homilies, sent it to Thorpe who confirmed that the language was 'saxon'.[4] The problem of seeing the manuscript had been solved meantime. The German antiquary, Warnkönig, having seen the account in the *Rheinisches Museum*,[5] writes to Cooper suggesting that a transcription should be made by Mone of Karlsruhe [6] and, upon his refusing, by Maier.[7] Maier left for Vercelli on October 15 1833 and appears to have completed his task in the spring of the following year.[8] The work was sent to Cooper, who was planning to print some of the manuscript as an appendix to the Report on Rymer's *Foedera* with which he was concerned as secretary of the Record Commission. At Thorpe's suggestion he decided to print all the verse [9] and Thorpe was asked to undertake the edition. The work seems to have been well advanced

[1] *Iter Italicum* i. 87, 99.
[2] Correspondence of Charles Purton Cooper iii. 104. The correspondence is now in the Library at Lincoln's Inn.   [3] *ib.* iv. 117, 126–9.
[4] *ib.* iv. 238, 273. Cooper seems to have sent specimens to Kemble also. See Correspondence v.248.
[5] *Rheinisches Museum für Jurisprudenz* iv. 233.
[6] Correspondence iv. 290.   [7] *ib.* iv. 298.
[8] *ib.* v. 322, 323. The transcript is now in the Library of Lincoln's Inn. Cp Ker, *Medium Aevum* xix. 17–25.
[9] *ib.* v. 463.

by 1835 [1] but the edition never appeared, for the Record Commission expired in 1837 and its report was not made. The appendices were stored and issued between July 8 1869 and October 10 1917 by the Record Office, which ordered that copies should be distributed in such a manner 'as may render them most useful for literary and historical purposes'.[2] A few copies, however, may have been distributed before 1869 and this is of interest for the history of the text, since Thorpe's work formed the basis of the early editions. Förster points out that Lappenberg seems to have received a copy, which he lent to Grimm who states in his preface that he made it the basis of his edition of *Andreas und Elene*, published in 1840.[3] Förster suggests that Lappenberg may have owed this copy to Thorpe, who was preparing a translation of Lappenberg's *Geschichte von England*. Grimm's edition was thus based on Thorpe's edition of Maier's transcript. Kemble's edition of 1843 seems to have been based partly on Grimm.[4] The first critical edition of all the verse in the codex was due to Grein but he, too, based his text on Thorpe, that is to say, on Maier's transcript.[5] Zupitza's

[1] Correspondence vi. 392.

[2] A list of recipients and details of distribution can be found in the *Printed Records Publications* of the Public Record Office i. 82; ii. 157, 158, 399.

[3] I have been unable to find any record of an issue of appendices A, B and C in one volume before 1869 although a copy of appendix B, which contains the text of *Elene*, was sent to Thorpe on November 23 1853. That Thorpe was accessible before that date is suggested by Grimm (*Andreas und Elene* p. iv) and by Kemble (*Poetry of the Codex Vercellensis* I v.). It may be suggested also by the existence at Lincoln's Inn of a second transcript signed *M.A.T. scripsit Ealing prope Londinium* 1835. The address and the initials suggest that it was made by one of Thorpe's family. Except for the runic passage from *Fates of the Apostles*, it contains the prose only and refers the reader to appendices B and D of Cooper's Report for the verse.

[4] See *Poetry of the Codex Vercellensis* I vi–vii.

[5] See Grein, *Bibliothek der ags. Poesie* i. 364. The inaccessibility of the manuscript vitiated some of the early discussion of the text, especially the cruces in line 580 where Thorpe, Grimm, Kemble and Grein read *awundrad* for MS *apundrad* and 1028 where they read *æðelu anbroce* for MS *æðelu anbręce*. Maier has the correct reading in 1028 and apparently *ápundrað* in 580 although the letters þ and p are difficult to distinguish in the transcript.

edition of 1877 was the first text of *Elene* to be based on a fresh inspection of the manuscript and incorporated a collation made by Professor P. Knöll of Vienna. All the poetry was collated by Wülcker for his revision of Grein. Other editors have used the collations of Napier or the facsimiles of Wülcker and Förster.

2. LANGUAGE OF THE TEXT

A linguistic analysis of the text of *Elene* suggests the following conclusions :

A. Certain features in the text are late West Saxon and are, therefore, scribal, since other evidence precludes so late a date. The most important of these forms are:

1. late WS smoothing appears in *ʒeseh* 841; *apehte* 304; *beþehte* 1298. These forms could, also, be Kentish or West Mercian, both dialects showing sporadic examples [1] (Bülbring § 313).

2. late palatal influence appears in *folcscere* 402; *ʒere* 859. Such forms are common in late WS (Bülbring § 314).

3. *frumþa* in 345 shows late *u* for *y*.

4. confusion of *u* and *eo* in *piðpeorþon* 294 (Luick § 286).

5. *e* in *hæftnede* 297; *þreanedum* 883; *perodleste* 63 etc may be due to a non-WS mutation of *ea* or to late WS shift of stress in diphthongs (Luick §§ 265, 266). Possibly due to the latter is *prohtherd* 494.[2] Cp *Andreas* 671.

6. *morðorslehtes* in 650 and forms such as *perʒðu* 211; *ermðum* 767; *herpdon* 387 etc may, also, show non-WS mutations but Ælfric's works show comparable forms [3] (Bülbring § 179 n.i).

7. *lixtan* 23 etc has *i* for earlier *ie*.

8. late WS labialization and delabialization are common throughout the poem.

9. *-an* for *-on* in *samnodan* 19; *lixtan* 23 etc.

10. *þane* for *þone* in 294.

---

[1] Cp *siʒe becna* with the *a* above the line in 974.

[2] Cp Schlemilch, *op. cit.* 24–6.

[3] Cp. Cosijn, *Altwestsächsische Gramm.* i § 14.

11. *-an/ -on* for *-en* in *ȝecyðan* 409; *piston?* 459 etc. But these may be dialectal forms.[1]

12. *-ade* for *-ode* in *locade* 87 etc. These are characteristically Anglian but occur also in late WS.

13. *-o* for *-u* in *snyttro* 154; *brimo* 971 etc.

14. irregular lack of syncope in *pereȝan* 357; *modcpaniȝe* 377 etc.

15. simplification of double consonants in *hetend(um)* 18, 119;[2] *niða* 503 etc; and lengthening of consonants in *fricȝȝan* 157; *bissceophad* 1211 etc (Luick §§ 667 ff).[3]

16. loss of final guttural in *pliti* 89. Such forms are common in Kentish glosses but occur in late WS also; cp the back spelling *reonian* for *reoniȝan* in 833.

17. loss of initial *ȝ* in *eorne* 322; *eáre* 399. This is characteristic of late southern texts (Sievers-Brunner § 212 n.2).

18. *pan næȝlan* for *pam næȝlum* in 1127.

19. *feale* for *feala* in 636?

20. *snyttro* is invariable in the singular.

B. The text shows some features common in early (Alfredian) WS. The most important of these are:

1. *meaht* 511; *meahton* 166 etc. These are either early WS or Kentish.

2. The diphthong *ie* in *dierne* 1080; and in *ȝeieped* 102; *hiehða* 1086.

3. the spelling *ie* for *i* in *hiere* 222; *biesȝum*(?) 1244.[4] This spelling is characteristic of the Hatton MS of the *Pastoral Care*.

4. the form *deoȝol* in 1092 has been regarded as Mercian but

---

[1] See Sievers-Brunner § 365 & n.2.

[2] This form, however, may be due to the influence of the related forms *hatian, hete, hetol*. Cp Beo. 1828; *Orosius* ed. Sweet (EETS 79) 264.

[3] Cp Dunkhase, *Die Sprache der Wulfstan'schen Homilien* 68–9.

[4] The *i* in this word has been added above and slightly to the left of the *e*. Most editors, therefore, regard it as a correction not an addition and read *bisȝum*. But additions without a tag appear in 954 and 731 where the *l* of *halfa* and the *o* of *siȝora* have been added above the line in the same way. No deletion point is visible under the *e* but the traditional reading may, perhaps, be justified by reference to *Andreas* 1286 where the reading *pelle* is corrected by writing an *i* over the *e* without a deletion point.

similar forms without the characteristic WS diphthong occur also in the Hatton MS of the *Pastoral Care.*

5. *dyrndun* in 626 may be an early form.

6. the spelling *sð* for *st* occurs in *oferspiðesð* 93; *ȝetæhtesð* 1074; *ricesða* 1234. This spelling is characteristic of the Hatton MS of the *Pastoral Care.* Since this manuscript was commissioned by King Alfred for Worcester, it was presumably written in a West Saxon scriptorium in his reign. Moreover, the spelling occurs in at least one other manuscript which can be shown to be descended from an Alfredian original; namely, the Cotton manuscript of Gregory's Dialogues, which seems to have derived from a copy made for Bishop Wulfsige of Sherbourne.[1] It is, therefore, possible that the sporadic appearance of this spelling betrays an early West Saxon transcript.[2] But since there are no other instances of this spelling in the Vercelli Book, the forms in *Elene* are more probably due to a previous transcript of the poem than of the whole codex which, in any case, probably did not take shape until the tenth century.

7. *byrð* 1195. Syncopated verbal forms may have become generalized in the late ninth century in the Winchester area (cp Sisam, *Studies* 125).

C. Dialectal forms common to the whole codex are probably to be regarded as scribal. These are forms showing *a* before *l* + cons. and the spelling *io*. Other dialect forms are probably poetic and, therefore, give no indication of the provenance of the poem. These are:

1. forms with back mutation of *æ* such as *beaduróf* 152; *heaðofremmende* 130; *eatol* 901 etc.

2. forms with back mutation of *e* before a dental such as *meotod* 366 etc.

---

[1] Sisam, MLR xviii. 254–6. For the forms see *Prologus* 13, 15, 18, 19.

[2] It is, perhaps, worth noting that several manuscripts showing this spelling are associated with the south-west; for example, Exeter Book (*Juliana* 53); MS C.C.C.C. 41, a manuscript once at Exeter (*Sol. & Sat.* 22, 36, 18); Corpus MS of West Saxon Gospels from Bath (Matt. xi, 7; xxiv, 39; xxv, 44). For forms in Canterbury Psalter and Rule of St Benet cp Wildhagen, *Stud. z. engl. Phil.* xiii 208, 159–72; Hermanns, *Interlinearversion der Benediktinerregel* 100. Cp Sol. Sat. ed. Menner 16–17.

3. forms with *e* for WS *ǣ*[1] such as *ȝeseȝe* 75; *neȝan* 287 etc.

4. reduplicating preterites as *heht* 42 etc; *leort* 1104.

D. Less common dialect forms, which may, in some cases, indicate the provenance of the poem, are:

1. irregular mutation in *prǣcmǣcȝȝas* 387; *sǣcȝ* ? 1256. Such mutations are frequent in Rushworth and Lindisf but not unknown in WS.

2. *stǣrcedfyrhðe* in 38 is probably Anglian.[1]

3. *ǣlfylce* in 36 may be Anglian but the prefix *-ǣl* occurs, also, in Hatton MS of the *Pastoral Care*.

4. *elda* 476; *heaðopelma* 579; *cearpelmum* 1257 represent forms occurring in Kentish, Saxon patois and sporadically in VPs.

5. second fronting appears in *hrefn* 110; *heremeðle* 550 etc. These are characteristically Kentish or West Mercian but occur sporadically in other dialects.

6. Anglian smoothing in *ǣht* 473.

7. (*feðe*)*ȝestas* 844 may be Anglian or Kentish.

8. (*puldor*)*ȝeofa* in 681 could be non-WS or Saxon patois.

9. *seolf* in 708 for late WS *sylf*.

10. *eorre* in 401 is Mercian and Saxon patois.

11. (*stan*)*ȝreopum* in 823 lacks the analogical restoration of *i* which is usual in WS.

12. *onsion* in 349 could be Northumbrian or Kentish but unmutated forms of this kind occur in Alfredian manuscripts.

13. Kentish or West Mercian fronting of *ǣ*[2] may occur in *elðes* ? 1294 and *stenan* ? 151.

14. Mercian confusion of *ð* and *d* in *ȝuðpearð* 14; *ȝehdum* 531; *elðes* ? 1294.

15. *ȝrinȝ* 115; *ȝrunȝon* 126; *ǣcleape* 321; *ǣclǣca* 901 show confusion of *c* and *ȝ* which occurs occasionally in R[1] but, also, in WS.[2]

16. *ástah* 188; *dreah* 1260 have final unvoicing which is common in R[1] but also in later WS; cp *purg* 289; 789.

---

[1] *ǣ* from mutation of *a* by retraction before *r* occurs in Northumbrian and in the Mercian Life of St Chad.

[2] Cp Campbell, *Battle of Brunanburh* 98, for the view that *crinȝan* and *ȝrinȝan* are from different roots.

17. West Mercian metathesis of *ðl* to *ld* in *spald* 300.[1]

18. nom. and acc. of personal pronoun appears in the plural as *heo* 116; 254; 382; *hio* 166, 324 etc; *he* 59, 68, 496.[2]

19. *hafu* in 807 and *pendo* ? 348.

20. *snyrȝan* for *snyrian* in 244.

21. *mid* with acc. in 275, 736, 997.

A linguistic analysis thus suggests that many features are late WS.[3] These presumably belong to the final stage of the history of the text, its incorporation in the collection represented by the Vercelli Book. Secondly, the poem shows some early features, some of them characteristic of the Hatton MS of the *Pastoral Care*, and the poem may at some time have existed in an early West Saxon form.[4] Finally, the balance of the occasional forms suggests a Mercian original. Of these the most significant is *spald*, the primacy of which is suggested by the metre, but the syntax and accidence of the poem would, also, support such a view.

The assumption that Cynewulf was a Mercian is confirmed by the metrical evidence. Most significant is the evidence of the leonine rhymes in the epilogue to which Sievers first drew attention.[5] These fall into three groups. Firstly, the rhymes *onwreah* : *fah* must be read as *onwrah* : *fah*. The form *onwrah* is more common in Anglian than in WS. Secondly, the forms *amæt* : *beȝeat* must be read as *amæt* : *beȝæt* or *amet* : *beȝet* if they are to rhyme.[6] The former would be non-WS; the latter would represent a second fronting dialect. Thirdly, the false rhymes *riht* : *ȝeþeaht* and *miht* : *þeaht* must be read as *ræht* : *ȝeþæht* and *mæht* : *þæht* or *reht* : *ȝeþeht* and *meht* : *þeht*. The rhymes *mæht* : *þæht* would show Anglian smoothing of *ea*; the *e* readings smoothing of *ea* to *e*. The latter is common in late WS but such an origin is impossible here. The only alternative is Mercian. The smoothing of *ea* to *e* occurs in VPs in such forms

[1] *seld* occurs in VPs and the Life of St Chad. Cp EPNS xxvi map 8.

[2] Cp Sievers-Brunner § 334 n.2.

[3] These late forms often vitiate the metre; e.g. *elþeodiȝe* 57, 82; *stiðhidiȝe* 121; *bepundene* 733; *hetend(um)* 18, 119; *niða* 465, 503; *eare* 399; *eorne* 322.

[4] Cp Sisam, *Studies* 12.

[5] PBB ix. 235 n.i.

[6] But see note to line 1247.

13

as *ʒepeht, bepehton, ʒepehte* and in R¹ in *ʒepehtunʒe*.[1] These rhymes, therefore, show only that the poet was Anglian.[2] The rhyme *ræht* : *ʒepæht*, on the other hand, could be only Northumbrian. Li. shows forms such as *cnæht*, but in other dialects the smoothing of *eo* is *e* and would give the form *reht*. If, therefore, it can be shown that the poet's dialect was not Northumbrian, the reading *reht* is necessary and the first rhyme is *reht* : *ʒepeht*. This would make probable a second rhyme *meht* : *þeht* although *mæht* : *þæht* [3] would be possible. But the forms (*ʒe*)*þeht* and *meht* are most probably West Mercian. The decision thus seems to lie between West Mercian and Northumbrian. That Northumbrian is, if not impossible, exceedingly improbable is suggested by the runic signature.

Sievers first noted that the poet's signature, fossilized in the acrostic, must represent the form which the poet was accustomed to use.[4] The variant *Cynwulf*, which occurs in *Crist* and the *Fates*, is current throughout the period, but the form *Cynewulf* must belong to a period during or after the transition of medial *i* to *e*. Since, moreover, the linguistic and metrical evidence suggests a Mercian or Northumbrian original, the evidence must be sought in dateable texts from these areas. The only available Northumbrian text, the *Liber Vitae* of the mid-ninth century, shows, in its many examples of the name, no form with medial *e*. It seems, therefore, that the evidence should be sought in Mercian texts. Dr Sisam has pointed out that the so-called Northumbrian genealogy, which Sievers used as evidence of *e* forms in Northumbrian, is, in fact, Mercian and witnesses the existence of *i/e* forms from the central midlands about the year 812.[5] The evidence of charters, upon which Sievers largely depended, is unreliable, since they are often preserved in later copies and their attribution may be untrust-

---

[1] But Lindisf and Ritual sometimes confuse *æ* and *e* and the smoothing of *ea* to *e* occurs sporadically in Kentish glosses.

[2] This conclusion is supported by the presumable rhymes *mæhte* : *cræfte* or *mehte* : *crefte* in *Jul*. 392 and *henþu* : *merðu* and *leht* : *neht* in *Crist* 591–2.

[3] The reading *æht*, adopted by many editors, does not affect the argument here; *æht* in 473 might be held to support *æ* forms, however.

[4] *Anglia* xiii. 11–15.   [5] See Sisam, *Studies* 6.

worthy. Relying, therefore, mainly on the evidence of the Northumbrian genealogy, it would be true to say that the runic signature suggests a date not earlier than the turn of the ninth century.

The conclusions from the linguistic evidence may be summed up as follows; the evidence of the occasional forms in the text suggest a late West Saxon copy of a West Mercian original through an early West Saxon intermediary. The rhymes, which are certainly Anglian, support the theory of a Mercian original, since it can be shown that the name *Cynewulf* makes a Northumbrian original unlikely.

3. THE SOURCE

The poem consists of a narrative followed by a personal epilogue. The theme of the narrative is the Invention of the True Cross, part of the medieval complex of legends about the Holy Cross. Of the four main groups, Inventio Crucis, Origo Crucis, Flagellatio Crucis and Exaltatio Crucis, the Invention legend is probably the oldest. The legends of the Invention and the Exaltation were closely associated with the festivals of the Invention and the Exaltation which, in the Roman church, were celebrated on May 3 and September 14, festivals which account for the frequency of these legends in the medieval Sanctuaria.

It has long been recognized that the source of *Elene* was the *Acta Cyriaci*, a version of which may conveniently be found in the *Acta Sanctorum* for May 4. This legend is probably of eastern origin [1] and combines the story of the finding of the True Cross by St Helena, a legend springing from the discovery of the Holy Sepulchre in 326, with the story of the hostility and ultimate conversion of a Jew called Judas. The development of the Helena legend can be clearly traced in patristic writings of the fourth and fifth centuries, while the history of Judas appears in the writings of the eastern fathers after about the middle of the fifth century.[2] Recensions of the *Acta Cyriaci* are

[1] See Straubinger, *Die Kreuzauffindungslegende.*

[2] For the development of the legend see Tixeront, *Les Origines de l'Église d'Édesse* 163–75.

widespread in Europe during the Middle Ages but the Greek and Latin versions may be regarded for our purpose as basic,[1] since it is most probably from them that the western vernacular versions immediately derive.[2] The Greek and Latin versions fall into well-defined groups.[3] The Latin texts, for example, form a group distinct from the Greek and Syriac texts because they alone have Judas as the brother of St Stephen. St Stephen Protomartyr could not, in fact, have been the brother of a Judas living in the time of Constantine, although he could have been the great-uncle of the traditional Judas Cyriacus, Bishop of Jerusalem, who suffered martyrdom in 134. Thus the relationship of great-uncle, which appears in most of the Greek and some of the Syriac versions, may be original [4] and the Latin version may have arisen, partly from the double reported speech, and partly from the double genitive in such a phrase as ὁ ἀδελφὸς τοῦ πατρός μου, which occurs in Vatican MS Graec. 866.[5] This, however, would imply a homogeneous development of the Latin versions, since they all have this relationship.

[1] The earliest versions were probably Syrian and the earliest extant text known to me is the Syriac text in B.M. MS Add. 14,644 which, according to Wright's *Catalogue of Syriac MSS in the British Museum*, is fifth or sixth century. Cp Nestle, *De Sancta Cruce.*

[2] This does not of course imply that the western versions cannot be indirectly influenced by the eastern versions. An instance of just such influence seems to be the dating of the Invention festival on May 7 in St Willibrord's Calendar (HBS lv) 29.

[3] For a list of known versions see Holthausen's 4th ed. of *Elene* and Dubois, *Les Éléments latins dans la Poésie religieuse de Cynewulf* 46–50. To these may be added for Greek: Bodleian MS Arch. Seld. B. 53, 54b; for Latin: Bodleian MSS Laud Misc. 129, 16b; *ib.* 238, 194; Fell 4, 208; Canonici Misc. 244, 57; B.M. MSS Royal 7 A. xi, 19; *ib.* 6 A. ii, 1b; Arundel 36, 50b; Egerton 2656, 179; Add. 11,880, 111; Cmbg. Univ. Lib. MS Mm. 6. 4, 229b. Bodley MS Canonici Graec. 19 ff 190b–197 contains a defective Greek text written probably in the fifteenth or sixteenth century. Since it is incomplete and late it has not been collated. Similarly an epitome of the *Acta Cyriaci* in B.M. MS Arundel 330 is too short to be of any value. Laud Misc. 129 and B.M. MS Add. 11,880 are more or less contemporary MSS but do not seem to have been the immediate source.

[4] Cp Ryssel, *Archiv* xciii. 8; Nestle, BZ iv. 336.

[5] See Wotke, *Wiener Studien* xiii. 302–11.

Secondly, the Latin texts never have the September dating of the Invention festival, which is common in texts of eastern origin, where it is probably due to its celebration, in the Nestorian church, on September 13, and in the Syrian church, on September 14. Moreover, the May dating, which properly belongs to the western versions, never appears in the Greek texts, although the date May 10 appears in Lauriotis' [1] text, where, however, it may have been taken from a Latin version. [2]

Thirdly, those Greek and Syriac texts which have Constantine's vision date it from the seventh and not the sixth year of his reign. All the Latin versions, on the other hand, have the sixth year. [3] Comparison of the Latin versions with the Greek and Syriac thus suggests that they developed within a homogeneous tradition, the characteristic features of which are to be found also in *Elene*, which must thus be supposed to have depended upon a version of this type and not, as has sometimes been thought, upon a version of the Greek type.

The dependence of Cynewulf on a Latin version is further indicated by the form of the *Hoptasia*, or vision of Constantine, which appears in *Elene*. Whether this motif was an original part of the legend is doubtful. The early Syriac text in MS Add. 14,644, dating from the fifth or sixth century, has no vision. On the other hand, the Rendel Harris codex, [4] from the eighth or ninth century, seems to have had this element, although not certainly, as the manuscript is defective at the beginning. That the vision is a later element is further suggested by the appearance, in Greek and Syriac versions, of the *Hoptasia*, without a date, but with a reference to the year of Constantine's reign in which the vision appeared. In these texts the date introduces the Invention narrative. In the Latin versions, on the other hand, the date introduces the vision. This suggests that the *Hoptasia* was a later addition, which, in

[1] See Ἐκκλησιαστικὴ Ἀλήθεια xx. 479–82, 494–6.

[2] No date is given in the abridged MSS B.M. Royal 7 A. xi and Arundel 36 nor in Canonici Misc. 244 and *Legenda Aurea*. Royal 6 A. ii is defective at this point.

[3] Except the defective Egerton MS. The figure is omitted in the abridged Arundel 36 and in the *Legenda Aurea*.

[4] See Nestle, BZ iv. 319–45.

the Latin texts, was welded into the story by the transference of the date to the new beginning of the narrative. The Greek and Syriac versions which have the *Hoptasia* without a date presumably represent an intermediate form. Moreover, the date in the Latin versions, 233,[1] belongs properly to the beginning of the Invention narrative, since it represents the number of years between the burial of the Cross under Trajan and its Invention. The addition of 117, the year of Trajan's death, gives a probable date for the Invention, A.D. 350.[2] The impropriety of the date at the beginning of the *Hoptasia* is emphasized by its conflicting with the dating of the vision in the sixth year of Constantine's reign. It thus appears that *Elene* must derive from a form of the legend in which the vision has not been simply added but incorporated by the transference of the date to the beginning of the text. This again points to a Latin text as the source.

The Latin texts themselves, however, can be grouped according to certain features in the narrative. Thus, the figures 3000 and 1000 which appear in lines 285 and 326 of the poem must be supposed to have been in the source. The number 3000, however, is omitted in Holder's Leiden MS and the motif is absent in Arundel 36 and the *Legenda Aurea*; the figure 1000 is omitted in Royal 7 A. xi and the motif in Arundel 36 and the *Legenda Aurea*. Similarly, the phrase 'two hundred more or less' (El. 634) appears as 233 in the Antwerp MS of ASS., Laud Misc. 238 and Canonici Misc. 244 while it is omitted in Arundel 36. None of these MSS, therefore, represent or derive from the source although they approximate to it in varying degrees.

Other considerations help to eliminate some of the remaining Latin texts. A small group only of these, namely Codex Maximinus of the *Acta Sanctorum* version, Royal 7 A. xi and the St Gall manuscript in Holder's collection,[3] has the baptism of Constantine by Sylvester which appears, also, in *Elene*. Con-

[1] Royal 6 A. ii and C.U.L. MS Mm. 6. 4 have 333: B.M. Add. 11,880 223. The figure is omitted in the defective Egerton MS. It is missing in Laud Misc. 238 and the *Legenda Aurea*.
[2] See Nestle, Gött. gel. Anz. 1880. 1530. MS Add. 14,644 has, in fact, 351. Cp *Calendar of St Willibrord* (HBS. lv) 29.
[3] See Holder, *Inventio Sanctae Crucis*.

stantine was, in fact, baptized by Eusebius of Nicomedia [1] and his name appears in many manuscripts. The baptism by Sylvester seems to represent a Roman tradition, although it appears, in two twelfth-century Greek manuscripts, Vatican MS Graec. 2048 and Lauriotis's text, where it may have derived from an earlier Latin version. Secondly, in Elene's second speech, the quotation 'Unto you a son is born' is attributed to Moses in the following Latin texts only: Laud Misc. 129 and 238, Mombritius, [2] Holder's manuscripts b c d, Egerton 2656 and B.M. Add. 11,880. Thus it appears that in a number of respects the St Gall manuscript 225 offers striking parallels with the text of *Elene*. In fact, collation shows that although in a few cases (for example, l. 90 ʒolde ʒeʒlenʒed clearly depends on the reading *litteris aureis* for which St Gall has *litteris*) other texts show closer readings, the St Gall MS may be taken as fairly representing the type of original upon which *Elene* was based. [3] This Latin text, resembling the eighth-century St Gall manuscript in Holder's collection, was perhaps already divided into numbered lections as are the Royal manuscripts. The lections in these two manuscripts correspond fairly closely with each other and with those in *Elene* and may have been traditional. The numbering of the lections in *Elene* can hardly have been the work of the scribe of the Vercelli Book, since they

[1] Eusebius of Nicomedia was an Arian. Hence, perhaps, the substitution of Sylvester, who is connected with Constantine's conversion in Ruffinus and other sources.

[2] Mombritius, *Sanctuarium* (Paris, 1910) i. 376–9.

[3] The St Gall manuscript although probably written at St Gall (see Lowe, *Cod. Lat. Antiq.* vii. 27) could have derived from an English original (cp Levison, *England and the Continent in the Eighth Century* 136 & n.1; 146). Of the ninth-century manuscripts, Add. 11,880 and Laud. Misc. 129, the former is much closer to *Elene* than the latter. Add. 11,880 was probably written at St Emmeram, Regensburg, in the first half of c. 9. It closely resembles St Gall 225 in its readings. See Bischoff, *Die südostdeutschen Schreibschulen* 207. It may be noted here that no source has been found for lines 966–1022 of *Elene* which describe how the queen sends messengers to Rome to report the finding of the cross to Constantine. Since, although the poet elaborates his material, he does not invent episodes except of the most conventional kind we should probably suppose that Cynewulf's original had some warrant for this passage.

occur only in *Elene*. The dating from the Nativity can be paralleled only from a Norse version,[1] which may indicate the existence of a Latin source with this feature, but more probably the coincidence is due simply to the authors' having worked within the same tradition.[2] Finally, it should be noted that attempts have been made to connect *Elene* with an Irish source on the basis of the spellings *Essaias* and *Ceruphin*, which Carlton Brown has shown to be common in manuscripts of Irish provenance.[3] The former occurs also in the Rushworth Gloss and in Lindisfarne, Matt. xiii, 14, and fifteen times in the *Pastoral Care*; the latter, in the form *cheruphim*, in *Andreas* 719 and, in the form *cheruphin*, in the Book of Cerne [4] and in the Canterbury Psalter xvii 11. Against this view it must be objected that the spellings are not necessarily original and, therefore, although they may indicate that the text was at some time copied in a scriptorium with Irish traditions, they cannot be used to show that Cynewulf used a Latin text of Irish provenance. In conclusion, it must be admitted that, with two notable exceptions, there is little in *Elene* which can be shown to be original. The exceptions are, of course, the elaboration in the epic manner of the battle scene and the sea voyage and, secondly, the epilogue.[5] For the rest, a glance at Holthausen's composite text shows that, poetic circumlocution apart, there is little which is not to be found in some version of the *Acta Cyriaci*.

The source of the epilogue may be considered under two headings: the precedent for the use of an epilogue of this kind

[1] See *Heilagra Manna Søgur*, ed. Unger i. 303–8.

[2] The Nativity dating may, however, be thought to favour an original which does not indicate its method of dating. Most Latin texts date from either the Passion or the Resurrection. Of those texts which have the figure 233 the following, however, have no such indication: Mombritius, Laud Misc. 129, Royal 7 A. xi and Holder a b (St Gall) c.

[3] ESt xl. 1–29; and on less solid grounds *Sachius*.

[4] Ed. Kuypers 85.

[5] There is one notable omission. All the Latin versions mention St Paul's trade. This is omitted in *Elene*. The twelfth-century manuscripts Royal 7A. xi, 6 A. ii and Arundel 36 give an abridged form of the text and omit this detail, but I have found no abridged versions before this period and the omission is no doubt Cynewulf's. Anglo-Saxon translators commonly omit technical details of this kind.

and the source of certain peculiar features in the account of the
Day of Judgement. The view that the epilogue is autobiographical and can be related to the vision celebrated in the
Dream of the Rood can no longer be seriously considered. The
epilogue seems to have a twofold inspiration: it is an acknow-
ledgement of the divine gift of poetry, which may have come to
the poet, as to Cædmon, in his old age;[1] it is, also, a prayer that
God will receive the poem as an acceptable service and a request
to the hearer to pray for the poet's soul. There is nothing
original either in the dedication of the poem or in the personal
tone, and parallels for both these aspects of the epilogue are
not far to seek. For example, the more or less contemporary *De
Laudibus Sanctae Crucis* [2] of Hrabanus Maurus is dedicated to
Christ and the saving power of his Cross, and in dealing with
such a theme the poet's thoughts turn naturally to the Day of
Judgement.[3] Bede, also, introduced the theme of Judgement
with a personal note of the same kind, describing how, solitary
and sorrowful, he was oppressed by his own sinfulness and
the thought of death.[4] These were sentiments common when
Cynewulf wrote, and there is no reason to suppose that the
epilogue is autobiographical. Moreover, there is a precedent
in Christian literature even for the combination of an epilogue
with a narrative, for a personal epilogue following a hagio-
graphical narrative is found in the *Vita Sanctae Mariae Mere-
tricis* of Ephraim of Edessa.[5] Like Cynewulf, Ephraim implies
that he is an old man burdened with sin, and he ends with a
prayer for mercy at the Judgement. It is not impossible that
the addition of such an epilogue to a saint's life was an imitation of Ephraim, since we know that the *Vitae Patrum* were

[1] This theme is conventional and appears, also, as is well known, in
the Preface to the *Heliand*.

[2] *De Laudibus* II xxviii (P.L. t. cvii col. 294).

[3] The transition from the Invention narrative to meditations on the
Last Judgement may have been suggested in part by the liturgy, since
the appearance of the Cross at the General Judgement is the theme of
versicle and response in the offices for the Invention of the Cross.

[4] *Hymnus de Die Judicii* (P.L. t. xciv cols. 633–8).

[5] *Vitae Patrum* (P.L. t. lxxiii cols. 659–60).

read in Ælfric's day [1] and there is some evidence for a wider knowledge of Ephraim's works in Anglo-Saxon times.[2] In any case, the parallel does at least suggest that the originality of Cynewulf lay less in the conception of an epilogue than in the combination of conventional themes.

The description of the Judgement has been thought to derive from chapter xxi of Alcuin's *De Fide Sanctae et Individuae Trinitatis*. Cook pointed out that *Elene* resembles Alcuin in two respects: the presence of purgatorial fire at the Judgement and the threefold division of mankind into *synfulle, awyrȝede womsceaðan* and *soðfæste*.[3] These characteristics are interesting, since they do not occur in other Old English Judgement scenes. Yet they are not peculiar to Alcuin but, as Carleton Brown has shown,[4] can be paralleled in a number of patristic writings. The threefold division, in particular, has a much closer parallel in Ambrose than in Alcuin, for Ambrose's division into *impii, peccatores, justi* more closely resembles the Old English than Alcuin's *impii, sancti, justi*; Ambrose, moreover, like Cynewulf, describes how the just pass through the fire unscathed. On the other hand, the parallel with Ambrose is not exact, for in *Elene* all rise to judgement, in Ambrose only sinners, since the just rise in the first judgement and the impious, who are judged already, rise to damnation.

4. DATE

Since attempts to identify Cynewulf with an historical figure have been unsuccessful, only internal evidence can be used for dating. The evidence may be summarized in this way: the date of the manuscript puts a terminus in the last half of the tenth century; the linguistic evidence a date not much before the early ninth century. This dating is supported by the order of items in the *Fates*, which seems to represent an order current

---

[1] Cp Aelfric's Latin preface to the *Lives of the Saints*.

[2] Grau thought that the epilogue was based on the Lamentations of Ephraim; see *Studien zur englischen Philologie* xxxi. 15–29. Cp Willard, MLA xlii. 329–30.

[3] *Anglia* xv. 9–20.   [4] MLA xviii. 308–34.

only after about 800.[1] If we accept the view that *Elene* was copied in a West Saxon scriptorium during the ninth century, however, the period during which the poem can have been written is greatly reduced. Attempts have been made to place the poem early rather than late on the grounds that in the eighth century the cult of the cross was particularly popular in England. But although the Invention festival seems to have been of Gallican provenance and does not appear, as is well known, in the Gregorian Sacramentary there is no evidence either that the cult of the Cross in general ceased after the eighth century or that the Invention festival was not known in England later in the Anglo-Saxon period. On the contrary, manuscripts such as the Leofric Missal, MS C.C.C.C. 270 and the Missal of Robert of Jumièges have proper masses for the feast and both Aelfric's account of the *Adoratio Crucis* [2] and the *Regularis Concordia* testify to the popularity of the cult. We hear of relics of the True Cross being presented to King Alfred in the ninth century [3] and of a Frankish mission in the tenth presenting to King Athelstan a magnificent gift consisting of relics associated with Constantine and the True Cross.[4] In favour of a ninth-century date it may, also, be pointed out that the acrostic was a most popular pastime among Carolingian scholars as the poetry of the period testifies.[5] At such a time Cynewulf would have been in the height of the poetic fashion in signing his poems in this way. Runes too were probably a fashionable study at this period.[6] The evidence, in fact, plainly suggests that Cynewulf was a West Mercian poet writing in the first half of the ninth century.

[1] Sisam, *Studies* 9.

[2] *Pastoral Letters*, ed. Fehr 161–4. Cp Brieger, *Medieval Studies* iv. 85–96.

[3] ASC. MS E 883; cp Stevens, *Yale Studies in English* 23.

[4] William of Malmesbury, *Gesta Regum* (RS) i. 150–1.

[5] Cp *Poetae Latini Aevi Carolini* (MGH, Poetarum Latinorum Medii Aevi 1–4) *passim*.

[6] Cp Derolez, *Runica Manuscripta* 217.

THE TEXT

The punctuation and use of capitals is modern and the text is printed in lines in the modern fashion. Square brackets have been used to indicate editorial additions. MS abbreviations and suspensions have been expanded without comment. The abbreviations and suspensions expanded are the tilde which is used for *m* and for *ne* in *þōn*, *þ̄*, roman figures for numerals, *ȝ* for *ȝeard* in 16, 774 and for *ȝe* in 1311, *7swēr* for *andsweredon* in 396, *scs* in 504, the w-rune for *wyn* in 788, 1089, *kł* for *kalend* in 1228. *7* is used as an abbreviation for the first syllable of *andsware* 166, 318, 375, 456, 462, 545, 619, 642, 662; *andwlitan* 298; *andsec* 472; *andweardlice* 1140.

CYNEWULF'S ELENE

þA þæs aȝanȝen   ȝeara hpyrftum
tu hund 7 þreo   ȝeteled rimes
spylce þrittiȝ eac   þinȝȝemearces
pintra for porulde   þæs þe pealdend Ꝥod
5 acenned pearð   cyninȝa puldor
in middanȝeard   þurh mennisc heo
soðfæstra leoht;   þa þæs syxte ȝéar
Constantines   caserdomes
þæt he Rompara   in rice pearð
10 ahæfen hildfruma   to hereteman.
Þæs se leodhpata   lindȝeborȝa
eorlum arfæst,   æðel[i]nȝes peox
rice under roderum;   he þæs riht cyninȝ,
ȝuðpearð ȝumena.   Hine Ꝥod trymede

TEXTUAL VARIANTS: (8) *Constantines*] Maier (prius ... *nus*). (12)
æðelinȝes] *æðelnȝes*.

(1) pæs: cp *Jul.* 678; *El.* 284–5; the singular may be due to the inversion or to the collective numeral. Cp Bauch, *Die Kongruenz in der ags.
Poesie* 52.

(2b) 'reckoning in numbers'. Cp *Phoenix* 29; *Genesis* 1335–6; *Andreas*
1035.

(3b) Cp *Andreas* 148. BT suggest 'measuring of time by events' but
the meaning is perhaps 'period of time'. *þinȝ* is cognate with Gothic
þeihs and the meaning 'time' is probably preserved here and in *þinȝ*
'assembly called at regular intervals'. See Hoops, *Reallexicon* s.v. *Ding*.

(11) Grein, *Bibliothek*, suggested *lindhpata* for *leodhpata* but emendation is perhaps unnecessary. *Leod-* may represent a fusion of the
variants *leoþu-/liþ-* with confusion between *ð* and *d* as elsewhere in the
manuscript (cp note to 522). Or *leod-* is possibly intensive; cp *reȝnþeof,
reȝnheard, dryhtenbealo, ðeodfeond*, although the latter, which occurs in
Wulfstan, may be due to ON *þjóð-*; cp Kock, ESt xliv. 393. Grein
suggests *leodȝeborȝa* for *lindȝeborȝa*; Holthausen, *Cynewulfs Elene*
(1910) *leodȝebyrȝa* after *El.* 203, 556; *Beo.* 269. But weak nouns derived
from verbal stems have mutation only if they are *-jan* stems and the
form in the text may represent a genuine unmutated variant. The word
means 'shield protector'. Cp *Germania* § 6.

15 mærðum 7 mihtum   þæt he maneȝum pearð
  ȝeond middanȝeard   mannum to hroðer
  perþeodum to præce   syððan pæpen ahóf
  pið hetendum.   Him pæs hild boden,
  piȝes poma;   perod samnodan
20 Huna leode   7 Hreðȝotan,
  foron fyrdhpate Francan 7 Hu[ȝ]as,
  pæron hpate peras
  ȝearpe to ȝuðe;   ȝaras lixtan
  priðene pælhlencan,   pordum 7 bordum

(21a) The *n* of *foron* seems to have been added later and a point inserted to separate *foron* and *fyrd*. (21b) *Huȝas*] *hunas*.

(17a) Cp *Beo.* 5. The functions of the good king are the consolation of the people and the confusion of their foes. Ekwall's reading *wra/æþe* (Anglia Beibl xxxiii. 65) is unnecessary.

(19a) Cp *El.* 71 'spefnes poma'. Etymologically *poma* is a sound or noise as in the cognate Lat. *vox* and OE 'pom 7 pop' in *Cr. & Sat.* 332. A secondary meaning 'noise of storm or battle' seems to occur here, in *Wand.* 103 and in ON *ómi* a *heiti* of Odin, god of storm and battle; and, perhaps, in *Ex.* 100; *Jul.* 136, 663. The meaning 'harbinger', 'one who speaks', is suggested by the cognate verb *peman* and by *dæg(red)poma* for the rising sun, or harbinger of day in *Guth.* 1218, 1292; *Andreas* 125. This sense is probably to be understood for 'spefnes poma' in *Dan.* 118, 538; *El.* 71. The phrase may derive from the medieval view of dreams as divine manifestations. Translate 'revelation of a dream'. Cp Schücking, *Untersuchungen zur Bedeutungslehre der ags. Dichtersprache* 91-8.

(20) For the Hreþgoths see Gradon MLR xlii. 161-72.

(21) The emendation *Huȝas*, first suggested by Zupitza, is supported by the association of these people with the Franks in heroic poetry. Cp *Beo.* 2910 ff.

(22) Klaeber, *Anglia* xxix. 271 'spylce Hetpare; pæron hpate peras'. For the Hetpare in association with the Hugas and the Franks cp *Beo.* But the half-line is complete in both metre and sense and, moreover, alliterates with the previous line. It may, therefore, be a metrical variant. Cp 371, 439, 451, 518, 582, 614, 1277.

(24b) Perhaps a corruption of 'ordum and bordum'. But the reference may be to some ceremony connected with the raising of the standard; cp *Ex.* 566-7. The clashing of weapons was a sign of assent (cp Tacitus, *Hist.* V xvii; *Germania* § 11) and it may have had other ceremonial uses: and the banners were sacred as representing images of sacred beasts and symbols of the gods. Cp Tacitus, *Hist.* IV xxii; *Germania* ed. Anderson 69-70. For ritual observances before battle see Amm. Marcell. xxxi. 7, 10.

26

25 hofon herecombol;   þa pæron heardinȝas
   speotole ȝesamnod   7 eal [syb] ȝeador.
   Fór folca ȝedryht,   fyrdleoð aȝól
   pulf on pealde,   pælrune ne mað;
   uriȝfeðera   earn sanȝ ahóf
30 laðum on laste;   lunȝre scynde
   ofer burȝen[de]   beaduþreata mæst
   herȝum to hilde   spylce Huna cyninȝ
   ymbsittendra   aper meahte
   abannan to beadpe   burȝpiȝendra.
35 Fór fyrda mæst,   feðan trymedon,
   eoredcestum   þæt on ælfylce
   deareðlacende   on Danubie,
   stærcedfyrhðe   stæðe picedon
   ymb þæs pæteres pylm   perodes breahtme.
40 Þoldon Rómpara   rice ȝeþrinȝan
   herȝum áhyðan;   þær pearð Huna cyme
   cuð ceasterparum;   þa se casere heht

(26) *syb* not in the MS. (31) *burgende*] burgenta. (35) Maier notes
three or four letters erased after *fór*. Now only a large stain is visible.

(26b) For the emendation see Sievers, Gött. gel. Anz. (1882) 997;
Grimm read 'eal speot ȝeador'. Perhaps a tribal name such as Spæfe or
Seaxe has been lost.

(31a) Early editors assumed a connection with *ent* 'giant'. Thus
Grimm read *burg enta*. Arngart, *English Studies* xxvii. 20–1, suggests
that the barbarians are gathering in an old castle. Grimm suggested
as an alternative *Burgendas* or *Burgendan* (Grein *Burgenta*) and this
view has been supported by Grattan, in MLR xv. 178, where he points
out that the Burgundians were near the Danube in the third century.
Objections to this are, firstly, that *Burgenda* would be the normal form;
but *t* and *d* are similar and the manuscript reading might exemplify a
common error, the substitution of a common for a proper noun as
perhaps in *Beo.* 1960, 1145; secondly, the function of *ofer* is then obscure
unless it is a noun and 'ofer Burgenda' means 'the banks of the Danube'.
But the intransitive *scynde* and the D half-line with alliteration on the
second lift tell against this. The text assumes *burgende* 'city boundary'.
For *ende* 'edge' see *Dream of the Rood* 29; *El.* 59.

(35–6a) 'the greatest of armies advanced—fell into formation—in
hosts'. The phrase 'getrym(m)ed feþa' glosses *cuneus*; see Wright-
Wülcker 216, 11–12; 110, 35.

onȝean ȝramum   ȝuðȝelæcan
under earhfære   ofstum myclum
45 bannan to beadpe,   beran ut þræce
rincas under roderum.   Þæron Rompare,
secȝas siȝerófe   sona ȝeȝearpod
pæpnum to piȝȝe   þeah hie perod læsse
hæfdon to hilde   þone Huna cininȝ.   fol. 121ᵇ
50 Ridon ymb rófne,   þonne rand dynede,
camppudu clynede,   cyninȝ þreate fór
herȝe to hilde,   hrefen uppe ȝól
pan 7 pǽlfel.   Þerod pæs on tyhte;
hleopon hornboran,   hreopan friccan,
55 mearh moldan træd,   mæȝen samnode
cafe to cease.   Cyninȝ pæs áfyrhted,
eȝsan ȝeaclad   siððan elþeodiȝe
Huna 7 Hreða   here sceapedon
ðæt he on Rompara   rices ende

(45) *beran ut:* probably intransitive. Cp ON *bera út*; *Andreas* 1221 and Kock, Lunds Universitets *Aarsskrift* (N.F. Pt. i) xviii. 22–3.

(50b–51a) For rhyme see Lefèvre, *Anglia* vi. 181–240; Kluge, PBB ix. 422–50.

(56–61) There are two difficulties here: 1. *sceapedon* in 58 does not agree with its apparent subject *cyninȝ*; 2. the MS reading 'ðæt he... samnode' implies that the antecedent of *he* is Constantine, which makes poor sense. *Sceapedon* has been explained as referring to both the king and the army (Körner, *Einleitung in das Studium d. Ags.* 269); to the scribe's having taken *elþeodiȝe* as the subject, as Holthausen (*Elene* 1936); or as due to a change of number (Klaeber, MPh iii. 449); or it has been emended to *sceapede* (cp ten Brink, AfdA v. 58). The latter may be supported by the Latin reading 'Videns . . . quia multitudo erat innumerabilis contristatus est ualde et timuit usque ad mortem'. But more probably *sceapedon* is intransitive. Cp Körner, *op.cit.* This use is not recorded but *seon* 'appear' occurs in Byrhtferth's Manual, ed. Crawford (EETS 177) 86, 8. *He* in 59 could refer to the Hunnish king, as Pogatscher suggested in *Anglia* xxiii. 289–90; or to *here* as suggested by Kock in ESt xliv. 394; or could be omitted as by Schaar in *Studia Neophilologica* xix. 312–13; Klaeber (ESt lv. 283) suggests that *samnode* is intransitive. But more probably *he* is plural (see p. 13) and the singular verb is due to scribal confusion. Thus read *samnodon* with ten Brink, *op.cit.* 58, and translate 'the king was fearful... when the barbarians...appeared because they had collected an army etc'.

(57) *egsan:* 'very'; see Schücking, *op.cit.* 35.

60 ymb þæs pæteres stæð   perod samnod[on]
   mæʒen unríme.   Módsorʒe pæʒ
   Rómpara cyninʒ,   rices ne pende
   for perodleste,   hæfde piʒena to lyt
   eaxlʒestealna   pið ofermæʒene
65 hrora to hilde;   here picode
   eorlas ymb æðelinʒ   eʒstreame neah
   on neapeste   nihtlanʒne fyrst
   þæs þe he feonda ʒefær   fyrmest ʒesæʒon.
   Þa pearð on slæpe   sylfum ætyped,
70 þam casere   þær he on corðre spæf,
   siʒerofum ʒeseʒen   spefnes poma.
   Þuhte him plitescyne   on peres hade
   hpit 7 hipbeorht   hæleða nathpylc
   ʒeyped ænlicra   þonne he ær oððe sið
75 ʒeseʒe under speʒle.   He of slæpe onbræʒd
   eofurcumble beþeaht;   him se ár hraðe,
   plitiʒ puldres boda   pið þinʒode
   7 be naman nemde—   nihthelm toʒlad—
   'Constantinus,   heht þe cyninʒ enʒla
80 pyrda pealdend,   þære beodan
   duʒuða dryhten;   ne ondræd þu ðe
   ðeah þe elþeodiʒe   eʒesan hpopan
   heardre hilde;   þu to heofenum beseoh
   on puldres peard;   þær ðu praðe findest
85 siʒores tacen'.   He pæs sona ʒearu
   þurh þæs halʒan hæs—   hreðerlocan onspeon—
   up locade   spa him se ár ábead,

(60) *samnodon*] *samnode*. (61) Maier read *moðsorʒe*. (69) The *p* in
ætyped has been altered from a *þ*.   (85-6) A point separates *ʒearu* and
þurh. (87) A tag is used to separate *se* and *ar*.

(65-75) Note the use of linked alliteration.
(71) See 19a.
(82) *hpopan* is subj.; cp *ʒecyðan* 409; *piston* 459; *ahenʒon* 475.
(86b) *Jul.* 79 suggests the translation 'he spoke'. See Ekwall, *Anglia*
Beibl xxxiii. 65. The subject of *onspeon* is probably to be understood
from *halgan* (cp *Anglia* xxiii. 280). In *Crist* 1055 *hreðerloca* is the part of
the body containing the thoughts. Cp *Elene* 1249.

fæle friðopebba; ȝeseah he frætpum beorht
pliti puldres treo ofer polcna hróf
90 ȝolde ȝe[ȝ]lenȝed; ȝimmas lixtan;
pæs se blaca béam bocstafum apriten
beorhte 7 leohte, 'Mid þys beacne ðu
on þam frecnan fære feond oferswiðesð,
ȝeletest lað perod'; þa þæt leoht ȝepát,
95 up siðode 7 se ar somed
on clænra ȝemanȝ; cyninȝ pæs þy bliðra
7 þe sorȝleasra, secȝa aldor   fol. 122ᵃ
on fyrhðsefan þurh þa fæȝeran ȝesyhð:—

.ii.

HEHT þa onlice æðelinȝa hleo,
100 beorna beaȝȝifa spa he þæt beacen ȝeseah,
heria hildfruma, þæt him on heofonum ær
ȝeieped pearð, ofstum myclum
Constantinus Cristes róde,
tíreadiȝ cyninȝ, tacen ȝepyrcan.
105 Heht þa on uhtan mid ærdæȝe
piȝend preccan 7 pæpenþræce,
hebban heorucumbul 7 þæt haliȝe treo
him beforan ferian on feonda ȝemanȝ,
beran beacen Ȝodes. Býman sunȝon
110 hlude for herȝum, hrefn peorces ȝefeah,
uriȝfeðra earn sið beheold
pælhreopra piȝ; pulf sanȝ áhof,
holtes ȝehleða; hildeȝesa stod.
Þær pæs borda ȝebrec 7 beorna ȝeþrec,
115 heard handȝespinȝ 7 herȝa ȝrinȝ
syððan heo earhfære ærest metton;

(90) *ȝeȝlenȝed*] *ȝelenȝed*. (91) Two letters have been erased before
apriten. (97) The last two letters of *sorȝleasra* on an erasure.

(106) 'arouse the warriors and hostility'. Zeugma.
(114) Compound subjects can take a singular or plural verb. But the
singular verb here may be due to the inversion. Cp *El.* 751, 892; Bauch,
op.cit. 60–2.

on þæt fæʒe folc   flana scuras,
ʒaras ofer ʒeolorand   on ʒramra ʒemanʒ,
hetend heor[u]ʒrimme   hildenædran
120 þurh finʒra ʒepeald forð onsendan.
Stopon stiðhidiʒe,   stundum præcon,
bræcon bordhreðan;   bil in dufan,
þrunʒon þræchearde;   þa pæs þuf hafen,
seʒn for speot[u]m,   siʒeleoð ʒalen;
125 ʒylden ʒrima,   ʒaras lixtan
on her[e]felda;   hæðene ʒrunʒon,
feollon friðelease,   fluʒon instæpes
Huna leode   spa þæt haliʒe treo
aræran heht   Rompara cyninʒ
130 heaðofremmende.   Þurdon heardinʒas
pide toprecene;   sume piʒ fornam,
sume unsofte aldor ʒeneredon
on þam heresiðe,   sume healfcpice
fluʒon on fæsten   7 féore burʒon
135 æfter stanclifum,   stede peardedon

(119) *heoruʒrimme*] *heora ʒrimme*. (124) *speotum*] *speotolū*. (126)
herefelda] *hera felda*.

---

(122) bordhreðan: cp *scyldhreoða*. *Sceldhreða* and *scyldreða* gloss
testudo and since *Exodus* 113 and 159 suggest that *bordhreða* and
scyldhreða were interchangeable terms, presumably *bordhreða* can have
this sense also, although it is usually glossed as *clýpei tegmen*. *-hreða*
is probably to be connected with *hreða* 'garment' and etymologically
bordhreða seems to mean 'shield covering' [cp *bordðeaca*] from which
it may be possible to assume a divergent development to *clýpei tegmen*
and *testudo*. Either sense would be possible here.

(124a) The MS reading is probably due, as Grein-Wülcker suggest,
to a blending of *speotum* and *speotole*. But *speotolum* might be a variant
of *speotole* as *miclum* : *micle*. *For* would then be a verb and the phrase
parenthetic.

(124b) Cp '*Carmen triumphale .i. imperiale* siʒarlic leoþ' in Napier,
Anecdota Oxoniensia (Mod. & Med. Series) 4 xi; 36, 1347. The etymo-
logical sense of *siʒe* 'magic', which is preserved in ME *siʒaldrie*, *siʒʒal-
dren*, is probably not intended here. *Jalan*, originally 'sing a spell', is
here best translated 'chant'. For the semantic association between
'cry' and 'charm' cp ModE 'charm'.

(134) fæsten: 'place of safety'. Cp *Maldon* 194.

(135) æfter: 'along'. Cp Norw. *etter*, dial. *after*.

ymb Danubie,   sume drenc fornam
on laӡostreame   lifes æt ende.
Ða pæs modiӡra   mæӡen on luste,
ehton elþeoda   oð þæt æfen forð
140 fram dæӡes orde;   daroðæs fluӡon,
hildenædran,   heap pæs ӡescyrded
laðra lindþered,   lýthpon becpom
Huna herӡes   ham eft þanon.
þa pæs ӡesyne   þæt siӡe forӡeaf
145 Constantino   cyninӡ ælmihtiӡ   fol. 122ᵇ
æt þam dæӡþeorce,   dompeorðunӡa,
rice under roderum   þurh his rode treo.
Gepat þa heriӡa helm   ham eft þanon
huðe hremiӡ—hild pæs ӡesceaden—
150 piӡӡe ӡepeorðod.   Com þa piӡena hleo
þeӡna þreate   þryðbord stenan,

(140) *daroðæs*] *daroð/æsc*.

(138–9) mægen...ehton: note false concord. The number of collective nouns is variable in OE; cp 231, 283, 762; Bauch, *op.cit.* 33–51.

(140b) daroðæs: if the MS reading is kept it represents either a compound noun as suggested by most editors and Klaeber, *Archiv* cxiii. 147–8; but *æsc* is masc. and cannot, therefore, properly be the subject of *flugon*; or asyndeton as Holthausen, Anglia Beibl. xv. 73–4 (cp Swaen, *Anglia* xvii. 124). Two consecutive nouns without a conjunction appear in Beo. 398, 1157, 1224, 1259 etc: but such collocations usually form a half-line. The reading in the text is Zupitza's *daroðas* with what may be a late spelling. But the scansion is irregular and the reading *daroð, æsc* is perhaps to be preferred.

(141) For *ӡescyrded* see AEW s.v. *scierdan*. Emendation is unnecessary.

(150–2) Cp *Beo.* 123–5.

(151b) There is no satisfactory solution of this crux. Körner (ESt ii. 254–5) tentatively equated *stenan* with NE stain and drew attention to a reference to coloured shields in *Germania* § 6. But apart from the contextual awkwardness there is no proof that *stænan* has a meaning other than 'to stone'. The meaning 'to adorn with jewels' assumed by some critics belongs properly to *astænan*. Moreover, although the Sutton Hoo shield and perhaps the obscure *staimbort* in *Hildebrandslied* 65 might be cited as evidencing jewelled shields, the phrase as a whole is still inexplicable. The identification with *stenan* 'to groan', 'to crash' first suggested by Körner is also contextually difficult. Sarrazin (ZfdPh xxxii. 548–9) emended to *þryðbold secan*. Perhaps we should

32

beaduróf cyninʒ   burʒa neosan.
Heht þa piʒena peard   þa pisestan
snude to sionoðe   þa þe snyttro cræft
155 þurh fyrnʒeprito   ʒefriʒen hæfdon,
heoldon hiʒeþancum   hæleða rædas.
Ða þæs fricʒʒan onʒan   folces aldor,
siʒerof cyninʒ   ofer sid peorod,
pære þær æniʒ   yldra oððe ʒinʒra
160 þe him to soðe   secʒʒan meahte,
ʒaldrum cyðan   hpæt se ʒod pære,
boldes brytta,   'þe þis his beacen pæs,
þe me spa leoht oðypde   ⁊ mine leode ʒenerede,
tacna torhtost   ⁊ me tír forʒeaf,
165 piʒsped við praðum   þurh þæt plitiʒe treo'.
Hio him andspare   æniʒe ne meahton
aʒifan toʒenes   ne ful ʒeare cuðon
speotole ʒesecʒʒan   be þam siʒebeacne;
þa þa pisestan   pordum cpædon
170 for þam heremæʒene   þæt hit heofoncyninʒes
tacen pære   ⁊ þæs tpeo nære;
þa þæt ʒefruʒnon   þa þurh fulpihte

(169) The last two letters of *cpædon* appear to be on an erasure.

---

read *ste(o)ran* (cp BT) and take *þryðbord* as 'mighty ship'. The confusion
of *n* and *r* is not uncommon. The ineptitude of the phrase in the context
is not without parallel in the poem.

(161b) Idiomatic use of *hpæt* with a masculine predicate. Cp 905
where *þis* is used with a feminine predicate. Cp Bauch, *op.cit.* 28–9.

(162a) 'lord of the palace'? Cp *boldaʒend*. *Bold* was probably an important building. It is used for the king's residence in Bede (ed. Miller
(EETS 95) 140, 22–5) and in a phrase indicating princely power in
Beo. 2195–6. Cp OE *heafodbotl* which translates Lat. *manerium*. Its
frequency as an element in place names may, also, indicate a building
of importance. Cp Ekwall, *Dictionary of English Place Names* s.v.
bóþl. Zupitza suggested emending to *blædes brytta*, Körner to *ʒoldes
brytta*. If the phrase is retained it should, perhaps, be taken as parallel
to *sigerof cyninʒ* in 158.

(172–6) The Latin *Audientes autem hoc pauci Christiani laeti* etc supports the translation 'when those who had been baptized heard that,
though they were few, their hearts were glad and their spirits rejoiced
that they might make known to the emperor the grace of the gospel'.

33

lærde pæron,   him pæs leoht sefa,
ferhð ȝefeonde,   þeah hira fea pæron,
175 ðæt hie for þam casere   cyðan moston
ȝodspelles ȝife,   hu se ȝasta helm
in þrynesse   þrymme ȝepeorðad
acenned pearð,   cyninȝa puldor,
7 hu on ȝalȝan pearð   Ȝodes aȝen bearn
180 áhanȝen for herȝum   heardum pitum.
Alysde leoda bearn   of locan deofla,
ȝeomre ȝastas   7 him ȝife sealde
þurh þa ilcan ȝesceaft   þe him ȝeyped pearð
sylfum on ȝesyhðe,   siȝores tacne,
185 þið þeoda þræce   7 hu ðy þriddan dæȝe
of byrȝenne   beorna puldor
of deaðe áras,   dryhten ealra
hæleða cynnes   7 to heofonum ástah.
Ðus ȝleaplice   ȝastȝerynum
190 sæȝdon siȝerofum   spa fram Siluestre
lærde pæron;   æt þam se leodfruma
fulpihte onfenȝ   7 þæt forð ȝeheold
on his daȝana tíd   dryhtne to pillan:—

.iii.

ÐA pæs on sælum   sinces brytta,   fol. 123ᵃ
195 niðheard cyninȝ;   pæs him nipe ȝefea
befolen in fyrhðe;   pæs him frofra mæst
7 hyht[a][h]ihst   heofonrices peard;

(186) The first three letters of *beorna* appear to be on an erasure.
(197) *hyhta hihst*] *hyht nihst*. (199) An *e* seems to have been erased after *cyðan*.

(184a) 'before his very eyes'.
(184b) 'by the token of victory'. The phrase is parallel to 183a. For the interchange of an instrumental with a prepositional phrase see Kock, ESt xliv. 394–5; Körner, ESt ii. 255. For the epithet see Patch, MLA xxxiv. 233–57.
(193) The unusual form *daȝana* may be a mistake but there is some evidence of weak forms of *dæȝ*; see BT, BTS *dæȝ*, Sievers, *Anglia* i. 577.
(197a) Emendations to *hyhta hihst* are on the analogy of *Guthlac* 63.

onȝan þa dryhtnes æ   dæȝes 7 nihtes
þurh Ȝastes ȝife   ȝeorne cyðan
200 7 hine soðlice   sylfne ȝetenȝde,
ȝoldpine ȝumena,   in Ȝodes þeopdom
æscróf, unslap. Þa se æðelinȝ fand,
leodȝebyrȝa,   þurh larsmiðas,
ȝuðheard, ȝarþrist   on Ȝodes bocum
205 hpær ahanȝen pæs   heriȝes beorhtme
on rode treo   rodora paldend
æfstum þurh inpit   spa se ealda feond
forlærde liȝesearpum,   leode fortyhte,
Iudea cyn   þæt hie Ȝod sylfne
210 ahenȝon herȝa fruman;   þæs hie in hynðum sculon
to pidan feore   perȝðu dreoȝan.
Þa pæs Cristes lóf   þam casere
on firhðsefan   forð ȝemyndiȝ
ymb þæt mære treo   7 þa his modor het
215 feran foldpeȝe   folca þreate
to Iudeum,   ȝeorne secan
piȝena þreate   hpær se puldres beam
haliȝ under hrusan   hyded pære,
æðelcyninȝes ród;   Elene ne polde
220 þæs siðfates   sæne peorðan
ne ðæs pilȝifan   pord ȝehyrpan,
hiere sylfre suna   ac pæs sona ȝearu,

(202) *æscrof* seems to be on an erasure.
(204) The last two letters of *ȝarþrist* appear to be on an erasure.
(221) *p* of *ȝehyrpan* above the line and a tag. (222) The *o* of *sona* appears to be on an erasure. The *p* of *pæs* has been added in the margin.

(205) It is not clear whether *beorhtm* should be regarded as a variant of *bearhtm*, *breahtm* (OE *brecan*; Corpus Gloss *braechtme*; Epinal *brectme*; OS *brahtum*). It is not usually recognized as such in the grammars. It may be an analogical reformation with the *e*-grade or due to confusion with *beorhtm*.

(212-14) Since *ȝemyndiȝ* with dative usually means 'memorable to' or 'worthy of remembrance by' we might here expect *ȝemyndiȝ* with a genitive, 'mindful of'. The translation, however, is probably 'Then was Christ's glory thenceforth present to the emperor's mind, concerning the Holy Tree...'; but Pogatscher (*Anglia* xxiii. 289) suggests that *pæs* is common to *casere* and *ȝemyndiȝ* which is possible.

35

pif on pillsið   spa hire peoruda helm,
byrnpiȝȝendra,   beboden hæfde.
225 Onȝan þa ofstlice   eorla menȝu
to flote fysan;   fearoðhenȝestas
ymb ȝeofenes stæð   ȝearpe stodon,
sælde sæmearas   sunde ȝetenȝe.
Ða pæs orcnæpe   idese siðfæt
230 siððan pæȝes helm   perode ȝesohte;
þær planc maniȝ   æt pendelsæ
on stæðe stodon.   Stundum præcon
ofer mearcpaðu   mæȝen æfter oðrum
7 þa ȝehlodon   hildesercum,
235 bordum 7 ordum,   byrnpiȝendum,
perum 7 pifum,   pæȝhenȝestas.
Leton þa ofer fifelpæȝ   famiȝe scriðan
bronte brimþisan,   bord oft onfenȝ
ofer earhȝeblond   yða spenȝas.
240 Sæ spinsade.   Ne hyrde ic sið ne ær   fol. 123ᵇ
on eȝstreame   idese lædan,
on merestræte   mæȝen fæȝ[e]rre.
þær meahte ȝesion   se ðone sið beheold
brecan ofer bæðpeȝ,   brimpudu snyrȝan,
245 under s[p]ellinȝum   sæmearh pleȝean,
padan pæȝflotan.   Þiȝan pæron bliðe
collenferhðe,   cpen siðes ȝefeah
syþþan to hyðe   hrinȝedstefnan
ofer laȝofæsten   ȝeliden hæfdon
250 on Creca land;   ceolas leton
æt sæfearoðe   sande beprecene,

(237) *Leton* on an erasure; *famiȝe* was written first with *æ* the second
stroke of which has been erased. (239) The last two letters of *spenȝas*
seem to be on an erasure. (242) *fæȝerre*] *fæȝrre.* (245) *spellinȝum*]
spellinȝum.

(230a) pæges helm: cp Riddle lxxvii. 1; Exeter Gnomes 73.
(245a) spellinȝ: 'swelling sail'. Although a *hapax legomenon*, this,
Thorpe's reading, is perhaps possibie.,
(245b) Cp Chaucer *shippes hoppestres.*
(251b) 'lashed with sand'. The emendation to *sunde*, supported by
Andreas 424, gives better sense. The suggestion is from Grein.

ald yð[h]ofu   oncrum fæste
on brime bidan   beorna ʒeþinʒes
hpone heo sio ʒuðcpen   ʒumena þreate
255 ofer eastpeʒas   eft ʒesohte.
Ðær pæs on eorle   eðʒesyne
broʒden byrne   7 bill ʒecost,
ʒeatolic ʒuðscrud,   ʒrimhelm maniʒ,
ænlic eoforcumbul.   Þæron æscpiʒan,
260 secʒʒas ymb siʒecpen   siðes ʒefysde;
fyrdrincas frome   foron on luste
on Creca land,   caseres bodan,
hilderincas   hyrstum ʒeþerede.
Þær pæs ʒesyne   sincʒim locen
265 on þam hereþreate,   hlafordes ʒifu.
Þæs seo eadhreðiʒe   Elene ʒemyndiʒ,
þriste on ʒeþance   þeodnes pillan,
ʒeorn on mode   þæt hio Iudeas
ofer herefeldas   heape ʒecoste,
270 lindpiʒendra   land ʒesohte,
secʒa þreate.   Spa hit siððan ʒelamp
ymb lytel fæc   þæt ðæt leodmæʒen,
ʒuðrofe hæleþ   to Hierusalem
cpomon in þa ceastre   corðra mæste,
275 eorlas æscrófe   mid þa æðelan cpen:—:   iiii.

HEHt ða ʒebeodan   burʒsittendum,
þam snoterestum   side 7 pide,
ʒeond Iudeas   ʒumena ʒehpylcum,
meðelheʒende   on ʒemot cuman

(252) yðhofu] yð liofu. (253) Maier bidan [prius bidam]. (279) meðel
heʒende] meðel/henʒende.

---

(252) Arngart, op.cit. 19 suggests yðliodu; cp leoþu Rhyming Poem 14.
But the traditional emendation to yðhofu 'ships', suggested by Gen. 1316,
is palaeographically more convincing.
(256–9) Cp Beo. 303–6, 1243–6.
(279) meðelhe ʒende: or her ʒende? cp BT. Confusion of r and n is not
uncommon in MSS. But the reading meðelheʒende, adopted by most
editors, is credible on the supposition that the scribe anticipated the

280 þa ðe deoplicost   dryhtnes ʒeryno
    þurh rihte æ   reccan cuðon.
    Ða pæs ʒesamnod   of sidpeʒum
    mæʒen unlytel   þa ðe Moyses æ
    reccan cuðon.   Þær on rime pæs
285 þreo þusendo   þæra leoda
    alesen to lare.   Onʒan þa leoflic pif
    peras Ebrea   þordum neʒan,
    'Ic þæt ʒearolice   onʒiten hæbbe
    þurʒ pitʒena   þordʒeryno
290 on ᴣodes bocum   þæt ʒe ʒeardaʒum
    pyrðe pæron   puldorcyninʒe,   fol. 124ᵃ
    dryhtne dyre   7 dædhpæte.
    Hpæt ʒe þære snyttro   unpíslice,
    praðe piðpeorpon   þa ʒe perʒdon þane
295 þe eop of perʒðe   þurh his puldre[s] miht,
    fram liʒcpale   lysan þohte,
    of hæftnede.   ᴣe mid horu speopdon
    on þæs andplitan   þe eop eaʒena leoht
    fram blindnesse   bote ʒefremede,
300 edniopunʒa   þurh þæt æðele spald
    7 fram unclænum   oft ʒenerede
    deofla ʒastum.   ᴣe deaþe þone
    deman onʒunnon   se ðe of deaðe sylf
    poruld apehte   on þera corþre
305 in þæt ærre líf   eopres cynnes.
    Spa ʒe modblinde   menʒan onʒunnon
    liʒe pið soðe,   leoht wið þystrum,
    æfst pið are,   inpitþancum
    proht þebbedan;   eop seo perʒðu forðan
310 sceðþeð scyldfullum.   ᴣe þa sciran miht

(295) *puldres*] *puldre*. (310) *scran* with *i* above the line and a tag.

---

participial ending. The lack of concord may be due to predicative use;
cp 992 and *JJJ* 19–21.

(293) The alliteration is probably *hp: p*; cp *Guth.* 263. The emendatior
to *ealre* (or *ealle*) *snyttro*, first suggested by ten Brink, *op.cit* .59, is thɪ
not essential although supported by the Latin 'omnem sapientiam'.

deman onȝunnon,   on ȝedpeolan lifdon
þeostrum ȝeþancum   oð þysne dæȝ.
Ȝanȝaþ nú snude,   snyttro ȝeþencaþ
peras pisfæste,   þordes cræftiȝe,
315 þa ðe eopre æ,   æðelum cræftiȝe,
on ferhðsefan   fyrmest hæbben
þa me soðlice   secȝan cunnon,
andspare cyðan   for eop[ic] forð
tacna ȝehpylces   þe ic him to sece.'
320 Eodan þa on ȝerum   reoniȝmode,
eorlas æcleape   eȝesan ȝeþreade,
ȝehðum ȝeomre   eorne sohton
þa pisestan   pordȝeryno
þæt hio þære cpene   oncpeðan meahton
325 spa tiles spa traȝes   spa hio him to sohte.
Hio þa on þreate   þusendo manna
fundon ferhðȝleapra   þa þe fyrnȝemynd
mid Iudeum   ȝearpast cuðon;
þrunȝon þa on þreate   þær on þrymme bád
330 in cynestole   caseres mæȝ,
ȝeatolic ȝuðcpen   ȝolde ȝehyrsted.
Elene maþelode   7 for eorlum spræc,
'Gehyrað hiȝeȝleape   haliȝe rúne,
pord 7 pisdom;   hpæt ȝe pitȝena
335 lare onfenȝon   hu se líffruma
in cildes had   cenned purde,
mihta pealdend   be þam Moyses sanȝ
7 þæt [pord] ȝecpæð,   peard Israhela,
"Eop acenned bið   cniht on deȝle

(311) on ȝedpeolan] 7ȝedpeolan. (318) eopic] eop. (338) pord not in
MS.

_____

(311) Ȝedpeolan could represent a case without a prep. or an adverbial
use. But more probably the abbreviation 7 stands for on; cp Gen. 1879;
Cr. & Sat. 502; Boethius, ed. Sedgefield 67, 24; Pastoral Care ed. Sweet
(EETS 50) 486. Cp Kock. Anglia xliii, 302; Klaeber, Anglia xxix. 271.
(320a) Either a B half-line with stress on þa or for 'þa on ȝerum
eodan' as Holthausen (Elene 1936) note to l. 320.
(339 ff) Isaiah vii, 14.

39

340 mihtum mære spa þæs modor ne bið
  pæstmum ʒeeacnod þurh peres friʒe."   fol. 124ᵇ
  Be ðam Dauid cyninʒ dryhtleoð áʒól,
  frod fyrnpeota, fæder Salomones,
  7 þæt pord ʒecpæþ piʒona baldor,
345 "Ic frumþa Ʒod fore sceapode,
  siʒora dryhten; he on ʒesyhðe pæs,
  mæʒena pealdend, mín on þa spiðran,
  þrymmes hyrde; þanon ic ne pen[d]o
  æfre to aldre onsion mine."
350 Spa hit eft be eop Essaias,
  pitʒa for peorodum pordum mælde,
  deophycʒʒende þurh dryhtnes ʒast,
  "Ic up ahóf eaforan ʒinʒne
  7 bearn cende þam ic blæd forʒeaf,
355 haliʒe hiʒefrofre; ác hie hyrpdon [m]e,
  feodon þurh feondscipe, nahton foreþances,
  písdomes ʒepitt: 7 þa pereʒan neat
  þe man daʒa ʒehpam drifeð 7 þirsceð
  onʒitaþ hira ʒóddénd, nales ʒnyrnpræcum
360 feoʒað frynd hiera þe him fodder ʒifeð:
  7 me Israhela æfre ne poldon
  folc oncnapan þeah ic feala for him
  æfter poruldstundum pundra ʒefremede":7

.v.

  HÞÆT pe þæt ʒehyrdon þurh haliʒe béc
365 þæt eop Dryhten ʒeaf dóm unscyndne,
  meotod, mihta sped, Moyse sæʒde
  hu ʒe heofoncyninʒe hyran sceoldon,
  lare læstan. Eop þæs lunʒre aþreat

(348) *pendo*] *peno*. (355) *me*] *þe*.

(345 ff) Ps. xv, 8.
(348b) Latin *commovear* suggests the emendation.
(353 ff) Isaiah i, 2–3. This text suggests Zupitza's emendation *eaforan ʒinʒe*.
(360) *Ʒifeð*: the singular is probably due to the indeclinable particle.

7 ȝe þam ryhte   piðroten hæfdon,
370 onscunedon þone sciran,   scippend, eallra dryhten,
7 ȝedpolan fylȝdon
ofer riht Godes.   Nu ȝe raþe ȝanȝaþ
7 findaþ ȝén   þa þe fyrnȝepritu
þurh snyttro cræft   selest cunnen,
375 ǽriht eoper   þæt me andspare
þurh sidne sefan   secȝan cunnen."
Eodan ða mid menȝo   mod[e] cpaniȝe,
collenferhðe   spa him sio cpen [be]béad;
fund[o]n þa fifhund   forþsnottera,
380 ales[o]n leodmæȝa   þa ðe leornunȝcræft
þurh modȝemynd   mæste hæfdon,
on sefan snyttro.   Heo to salore eft
ymb lytel fæc   laðode pæron,
ceastre peardas;   hio sio cpen onȝan
385 pordum ȝeneȝan—   plat ofer ealle—
'Oft ȝe dyslice   dæd ȝefremedon,
perȝe præcmæcȝȝas   7 ȝepritu herpdon,
fædera lare   næfre furður þonne nu   fol. 125ª
ða ȝe blindnesse   bote forseȝon
390 7 ȝe piðsocon   soðe 7 rihte,
þæt in Bethleme   bearn pealdendes,
cyninȝ ánboren   cenned pære,
æðelinȝa ord;   þeah ȝe þa ǽ cuðon,

(377) *mode cpaniȝe*] mod cpaniȝe. (378) *bebead*] bead. (379) *fundon*]
funden. (380) *aleson*] alesen. (392) *pære*] pære pære.

(369b) *piðreotan* is a *hapax legomenon*. Since *piþ* is usually adversative
it presumably means 'be averse from', 'oppose'. This meaning is confirmed by the OHG gloss *aborret uuidharruzzit*; see Grein-Köhler, s.v.
wiðreotan.

(370) Most editors insert either *dryhtna* or *duȝuða* before *dryhten*
and read a full line with D alliteration in 371. But line 370 is made up
of parallel epithets like 1042. *Sciran* may be substantival, as *beorhtan*
in 782, or attributive. For scansion cp 891.

(377b) 'sad at heart'. Editors emend to *mode(s)cpan(i)ȝe*; Holthausen
(*Anglia* xxiii. 516) *modcpanȝe ȝuman*. The evidence of the rest of the
poem suggests that the spellings -*iȝe* for -*ȝe* are scribal, since they often
give a dissyllabic second sinking. Cp 57, 82, 121, 166, 314, 355, 478, 560,
762, 847, 977, 1214.

41

pitȝena þord   ȝe ne poldon þa,
395 synpyrcende   soð oncnapan.'
Hie þa ánmode   andsperedon,
'Hpæt þe Ebreisce   ǽ leornedon
þa on fyrndaȝum   fæderas cuðon
æt Ȝodes earce   ne þe eare cunnon
400 þurh hpæt ðu ðus hearde,   hlæfdiȝe, us
eorre purde;   þe ðæt ǽbylȝð nyton
þe þe ȝefremedon   on þysse folcscere,
þeodenbealpa   þið þec æfre'.
Elene maðelade   7 for eorlum spræc,
405 undearninȝa   ides reordode,
hlude for heriȝum,   'Ȝe nu hraðe ȝanȝað,
sundor ásecaþ   þa ðe snyttro mid eop,
mæȝn 7 modcræft   mæste hæbben
þæt me þinȝa ȝehpylc   þriste ȝecyðan,
410 untraȝlice   þe ic him to sece'.
Eodon þa fram rune   spa him sio rice cpen,
bald in burȝum   beboden hæfde,
ȝeomormode   ȝeorne smeadon,
sohton searoþancum   hpæt sio syn pære
415 þe hie on þam folce   ȝefremed hæfdon
þið þam casere   þe him sio cpen pite.
Þa þær for eorlum   án reordode,
ȝidda ȝearosnotor   ðam pæs Iudas nama,
þordes cræftiȝ,   'Ic þat ȝeare
420 þæt hio þile secan   be ðam siȝebeame
on ðam þropode   þeoda paldend
eallra ȝnyrna leas,   Ȝodes aȝen bearn
þone [or]scyld[ne]   eofota ȝehpylces

(394) *e* of *pitȝena* above the line and a tag. (401) Maier reads *æby*
(*r* erasū) *lgð*. A point is used to connect the parts of the word separated
by the erasure. (411) *cpen* on an erasure. (422) *ȝnyrna*] *ȝnyrnra*. (423)
orscyldne] *scyldū*.

(401–3) æbylgð . . . þeodenbealpa: note the double construction
after *þitan ;* cp Kock, ESt xliv. 395; Kern, ESt li. 11.
(409) ȝecyðan: see note to line 82.
(423) For the emendation see Trautmann (BB xxiii. 99).

þurh hete henȝon   on heanne beam
425 in fyrndaȝum   fæderas usse.
Þæt pæs þrealic ȝeþoht!   Nu is þearf mycel
þæt pe fæstlice ferhð staðelien
þæt pe ðæs morðres   meldan ne peorðen
hpær þæt haliȝe trio   beheled purde
430 æfter piȝþræce   þylæs toporpen sien
frod fyrnȝepritu   7 þa fæderlican
lare forlet[e]n.   Ne bið lanȝ ofer ðæt
þæt Israhela   æðelu moten
ofer middanȝeard   má ricsian,
435 æcræft eorla   ȝif ðis yppe bið.
Spa þa þæt ilce ȝio   mín yldra fæder
siȝerof sæȝde—   þam pæs Sachius nama—
frod fyrnpiota   fæder minum,
[fæder min] eaferan;
440 pende hine of porulde   7 þæt pord ȝecpæð,
"Gif þe þæt ȝelimpe   on lifdaȝum
þæt ðu ȝehyre   ymb þæt haliȝe treo
frode friȝnan   7 ȝeflitu ræran   fol. 125ᵇ
be ðam siȝebeame   on þam soðcyninȝ
445 ahanȝen pæs,   heofonrices peard,
eallre sybbe bearn,   þonne þu snude ȝecyð,
mín spæs sunu,   ær þec spylt nime.
Ne mæȝ æfre ofer þæt   Ebrea þeod,
rædþeahtende   rice healdan,
450 duȝuðum pealdan   ac þara dom leofað
7 hira dryhtscipe
in poruld peorulda   pillum ȝefylled
ðe þone ahanȝnan cyninȝ   heriaþ 7 lofiað":—

---

(424) A comma erased above and to the right of *þurh*. (432) *forleten*]
forleton. (439) *fæder min* not in MS. (453) *ðe* above the line and tag.

(432a) The MS reading may represent a nWS form of the past participle; cp Sievers-Brunner § 366, 2 and line 971.

(438-9) The Latin has 'Avus meus praenuntiavit patri meo et pater meus...adnuntiavit mihi dicens'... The emendation is based on the assumption that the Old English had a similar expression which was omitted by haplography. The construction is asyndetic. For the scansion see PBB x. 483 and Das, *Cynewulf and the Cynewulf Canon* pp. 27, 125.

43

.vi.

ÞA ic fromlice fæder minum,
455 ealdum æpitan aȝeaf andspare,
"Hu polde þæt ȝepeorðan on poruldrice
þæt on þone halȝan handa sendan
to feorhleȝe fæderas usse
þurh prað ȝepitt ȝif hie piston ǽr
460 þæt he Crist pære, cyninȝ on roderum,
soð sunu meotudes, sapla nerȝend?"
Ða me yldra mín aȝeaf andspare,
fród on fyrhðe fæder reordode,
"Onȝit ȝuma ȝinȝa Ȝodes heahmæȝen,
465 nerȝendes naman se is niða ȝehpam
unasecȝendlic þone sylf ne mæȝ
on moldpeȝe man aspyriȝean.
Næfre ic þa ȝeþeahte þe þeos þeod onȝan
secan polde ac ic symle mec
470 ásced þara scylda, nales sceame porhte
ȝaste minum; ic him ȝeorne oft
þæs unrihtes andsæc fremede
þonne uðpeotan æht bisæton,
on sefan sohton hu hie sunu meotudes
475 áhenȝon, helm pera, hlaford eallra
enȝla 7 elda, æðelust bearna.
Ne meahton hi[m] spa disiȝe deað oðfæstan
peras ponsæliȝe spa hie pendon ær,
sarum settan, þeah he sume hpile
480 on ȝalȝan his ȝast onsende,
siȝebearn Godes; þa siððan pæs
of rode ahæfen rodera pealdend,
eallra þrymma þrym; þreo niht siððan
in byrȝenne bidende pæs
485 under þeosterlocan 7 þa þy þriddan dæȝ
(477) *him*] *hie.*

---

(459) piston: see note to line 82.
(475) áhenȝon: see note to line 82.

44

ealles leohtes leoht   lifȝende áras,
ðeoden enȝla   7 his þeȝnum,
soð siȝora frea   seolfne ȝeypde,
beorht on blæde;   þonne broðor þin
490 onfenȝ æfter fyrste   fulpihtes bæð,
leohtne ȝeleafan;   þa for lufan dryhtnes
Stephanus þæs   stanum porpod;
ne ȝeald he yfel yfele   ac his ealdfeondum
þinȝode þrohtherd,   bæd þrymcyninȝ
495 þæt he him þa peadæd   to præce ne sette
þæt he for æfstum   unscyldiȝne,
synna leasne   Saples larum
feore beræddon;   spa he þurh feondscipe   fol. 126ᵃ
to cpale moniȝe   Cristes folces
500 demde to deaþe   spa þeah him dryhten eft
miltse ȝefremede   þæt he maneȝum [pearð]
folca to frofre;   syððan him frymða ȝod,
niða nerȝend   naman oncyrde
7 he syððan þæs   Sanctus Paulus
505 be naman haten   7 him næniȝ þæs
ǽlærendra   oðer betera
under speȝles hleo   syðþan æfre
þara þe pif oððe per   on poruld cendan
þeah he Stephanus   stanum hehte
510 ábreotan on beorȝe,   broðor þinne.
Nu ðu meaht ȝehyran,   hæleð mín se leofa,
hu árfæst is   ealles pealdend
þeah pe ǽbylȝð pið hine   oft ȝepyrcen,
synna punde   ȝif þe sona eft
515 þara bealudæda   bote ȝefremmaþ
7 þæs unrihtes   eft ȝespicaþ.
Forðan ic soðlice   7 mín spæs fæder

(501) *pearð* not in MS.

(487b) The MS reading gives a very weak half-line with vowel alliteration. Dr Brooks has suggested to me that the correct reading is '7 þeȝnum his' which seems probable.

(508) Note the lack of concord. For the congruence of compound subjects see Bauch, *op.cit.* 63.

syðþan ʒelyfdon
þæt ʒeþropade eallra þrymma Ʒod,
520 lifes láttiop laðlic píte
for oferþearfe ilda cynnes.
Forðan ic þe lære þurh leoðorune,
hyse leofesta, þæt ðu hospcpide,
æfst ne eofulsæc æfre ne fremme,
525 ʒrimne ʒeaʒncpide pið Ʒodes bearne;
þonne ðu ʒeearnast þæt þe bið ece líf,
selust siʒeleana seald in heofonum.'
Ðus mec fæder mín on fyrndaʒum
unpeaxenne pordum lærde,
530 septe soðcpidum— þam pæs Symon nama—
ʒuma ʒehdum fród. Nu ʒe ʒeare cunnon
hpæt eop þæs on sefan selest þince
to ʒecyðanne ʒif ðeos cpen usic
friʒneð ymb ðæt treo nu ʒe fyrhðsefan
535 7 modʒeþanc minne cunnon'.
Him þa toʒenes þa ʒleapestan
on pera þreate pordum mældon,
'Næfre we hyrdon hæleð æniʒne
on þysse þeode butan þec nuða,
540 þeʒn oðerne þyslic cyðan
ymb spa dyʒle pyrd; do spa þe þynce,

(524) Maier thought that two letters, perhaps *ne*, had been erased
after *fremme*. (526) Two letters, read by Maier as *ya?*, erased before
ece. (531) An erasure after *fród*.

(521) oferþearfe: 'great need'. The use of *ofer-* in this sense may be
due to Latin influence. See Baxter and Johnson, *Medieval Latin Word-
List* s.v. *super-*.

(522) leoðorune: cp 1250 *leoðucræft*; the emended forms *leoðrune,
leoðcræft* are probably to be preferred although the form *leoðocræft*
may be compared with *leoðufæst* 'skilful'. Cp *Beo.* 2769, *leoðocræftum*
'skilfully'.

(531) gehdum: Zupitza emended to *giddum* but the phrase may mean
'well-versed in sorrow', 'wise'; cp *Beo.* 3095 and Klaeber, ESt lv. 284;
Kern, *Taalkundige Bijdragen* i. 208-9.

(534a) For the scansion see Klaeber, *Beowulf* (1941) p. 279. But the
line is readily emended to *ymb ðæt treo friʒneð*.

fyrnȝidda frod,   ȝif ðu fruȝnen sie
on pera corðre.   Þisdomes beðearf,
porda pærlicra   7 pitan snyttro
545 se ðære æðelan sceal   andpyrde aȝifan
for þyslicne   þreat on meþle':7

.vii.

ÞEOXan pordcpidum,   peras þeahtedon
on healfa ȝehpær   sume hyder sume þyder,
þrydedon 7 þohton;   þa cpom þeȝna heap
550 to þam heremeðle,   hreopon friccan,
caseres bodan,   'Eop þeos cpen laþaþ,   fol. 126b
secȝas to salore   þæt ȝe seonoðdomas
rihte reccen;   is eop rædes þearf,
on meðelstede   modes snyttro'.
555 Heo pæron ȝearpe,   ȝeomormode
leodȝebyrȝean   þa hie laðod pæron
þurh heard ȝebann;   to hofe eodon,
cyðdon cræftes miht.   Þa sio cpen onȝan
peras Ebresce   pordum neȝan,
560 fricȝȝan fyrhðperiȝe   ymb fyrnȝepritu
hu on porulde ær   pitȝa[n] sunȝon,
ȝasthaliȝe ȝuman   be Ȝodes bearne
hpær se þeoden   ȝeþropade,
soð sunu meotudes   for sapla lufan.
565 Heo pæron stearce,   stane heardran,
noldon þæt ȝeryne   rihte cyðan
ne hire andspare   æniȝe secȝan,
tornȝeniðlan   þæs hio him to sohte

(561) pitȝan] pitȝa.

(547a) Cosijn, *Tijdschrift voor Nederlandsche Taal- en Letterkunde* i 144 reads *prixledan* supposing confusion arose from an original northern *peoxledan*; cp *prixlan ȝiddum*; *pordum prixlan*. But the idiom here is not impossible. Grimm compares *Heliand* 5969 f. 'bigunnun im quidi managa wahsan'. The subject however is 'they' not 'words', since the metre requires *pordcpidum* as a compound. *Arngart (op.cit.* 20) compares M.N.D. II i. 56 '(they) waxen in their mirth'.

ac hio þorda ʒehþæs   piðersæc fremedon,
570 fæste on fyrhðe   þæt heo friʒnan onʒan,
cpædon þæt hio on aldre   opiht spylces
ne ær ne sið   æfre hyrdon.
Elene maþelade   7 him yrre oncpæð,
'Ic eop to soðe   secʒan pille
575 7 þæs in life   liʒe ne pyrðeð
ʒif ʒe þissum lease   lenʒ ʒefylʒað,
mid fæcne ʒefice,   þe me fore standaþ
þæt eop in beorʒe   bǽl fornimeð,
hattost heaðopelma   7 eoper hra bryttað,
580 lacende liʒ   þæt eop sceal þæt leas ápundrad
peorðan to poruldʒedale.   Ne maʒon ʒe ða þord
ʒeseðan
þe ʒe hpile nú on unriht
priʒon under þomma sceatum;   ne maʒon ʒe þa pyrd
bemiðan,
bedyrnan þa deopan mihte'.   Ða þurdon hie deaðes
on þenan,
585 ádes 7 endelifes   7 þær þa ænne betæhton
ʒiddum ʒearusnottorne—   þam þæs Iudas nama
cenned for cneomaʒum—   þone hie þære cpene aʒefon,
sæʒdon hine sundorpisne,   'He þe mæʒ soð ʒecyðan,
onþreon pyrda ʒeryno   spa ðu hine þordum friʒnest,
590 ǽriht from ord[e]   oð ende forð;

(590) orde] ord.

(578b) Frucht's reading 'bælfyr nimeð' is unnecessary (Metrisches u. Sprachliches zu Cy's El. 30). Cp Ælfric Hom. ed. Thorpe i. 322: 'God is spa spa Paulus cpæð, fornymende fyr' from Heb. xii, 29 'Etenim deus noster ignis consumens est'. For the scansion see PBB x. 230-2.

(580) Thorpe's false reading apundrad for the MS. apundrad, was adopted as an emendation by Grein-Wülcker; Grimm suggested apended; Strunk, MLN xvii. 373, asundrad. But apundrad may mean 'considered'. Pundernian and apyndrian seem to mean 'weigh', but the metaphorical sense appears in pundere 'scholar'; OF ponderer, whence ModE 'ponder', may have merely reinforced an existing sense of an OE apundrian. Translate 'that lie shall be accounted to you worthy of death'? Most editors end line 580 after leas but a half-line makes this unnecessary.

(590) orde oð ende: cp Onions, MLR xxiv. 389–93.

he is for eorðan   æðeles cynnes,
þordcræftes þis   7 þitȝan sunu,
bald on meðle;   him ȝebyrde is
þæt he ȝencþidas   ȝleaþe hæbbe,
595   cræft in breostum;   he ȝecyðeð þe
for þera menȝo   þisdomes ȝife
þurh þa myclan miht   spa þín mod lufaþ'.
Hio on sybbe forlet   secan ȝehþylcne
aȝenne eard   7 þone ænne ȝenam
600   Iudas to ȝisle   7 þa ȝeorne bæd   fol. 127ᵃ
þæt he be ðære rode   riht ȝetæhte
þe ær in leȝere þæs   lanȝe bedyrned
7 hine seolfne   sundor aciȝde.
Elene maþelode   to þam ánhaȝan,
605   tíreadiȝ cþen,   'þe synt tu ȝearu,
spa líf spa deað   spa þe leofre bið
to ȝeceosanne;   cyð ricene nu
hpæt ðu þæs to þinȝe   þafian þille'.
Iudas hire onȝen þinȝode—   ne meahte he þa ȝehðu
      bebuȝan,
610   oncyrran [cyninȝ] ȝeniðlan,   he pæs on þære cþene
      ȝeþealdum—
'Hu mæȝ þæm ȝeþeorðan   þe on þestenne
meðe 7 meteleas   mórland trydeð,
hunȝre ȝehæfted   7 him hlaf 7 stan
on ȝesihðe bú ȝeþeorðað
615   stea[r]c 7 hnesce,   þæt he þone stan nime
þið hunȝres hleo,   hlafes ne ȝime,

---

(599) an erasure after the first *n* of *aȝenne*.
(610) *cyninȝ*] *rex*. (615) *stearc*] *streac*.

---

(608) *þæs to þinȝe*: 'as a condition', viz. 'which alternative will you choose?'

(610) For the reading *cyninȝ* see Holthausen, Anglia Beibl xxi. 174. Cp 1041.

(614) Most editors add a word before *ȝeþeorðað*; Zupitza suggests *samod ȝeþeorðað*; Klaeber, JEGP xviii. 252 *ȝeseted þeorðað*.

(615) For the form *streac* compare *Andreas* 196 *sæstearmas*; and, perhaps, *Andreas* 1313 *ȝescyrded*.

ȝepende to pædle   7 þa piste piðsæce,
beteran piðhyccȝe   þonne he beȝa beneah':—

.viii.

HIM þa seo eadiȝe   andpyrde áȝeaf,
620 Elene for eorlum   undearnunȝa,
'Gif ðu in heofonrice   habban pille
eard mid enȝlum   7 on eorðan líf,
siȝorlean in speȝle,   saȝa ricene me
hpær seo rod puniȝe   radorcyninȝes,
625 haliȝ under hrusan   þe ȝe hpile nú
þurh morðres mán   mannum dyrndun.'
Iudas maðelade—   him pæs ȝeomor sefa,
hat æt heortan   7 ȝehpæðres pá
ȝe h[im] heofonrices   [hador] spamode,
630 7 þis andpearde   ánforlete,
rice under roderum,   ȝ[if] he ða rode ne tæhte—
'Hu mæȝ ic þæt findan   þæt spa fyrn ȝepearð
pintra ȝanȝum?   Is nu porn sceacen
tu hund oððe ma   ȝeteled rime;
635 ic ne mæȝ areccan   nu ic þæt rim ne can;

(629a) *him*] *he*. (629b) *hador* not in MS. (631) *ȝif*] *ȝe*.

(628–31) The Latin has 'Si ergo in caelo et in terra vis vivere, dic mihi, ubi absconditum est lignum pretiosae crucis'. The sense of the English is thus that, if Judas conceals the whereabouts of the cross, his affliction will be twofold: his body will die and his soul will perish in hell. *Ȝe* in 631 is thus inappropriate and Trautmann's reading *ȝif* in BB xxiii. 103 has been adopted. MS *spamode* could represent a verb *spæman* by confusion of *spa* and *spæ*, for, although the simplex does not occur in OE, ME *spemen* suggests a transitive verb 'grieve'. It would then be possible to keep MS *he* and read 'ȝe he heofonrices hlaford spæmde'. But the reading in the text, an adaptation of Zupitza's 'hyht spæmode', has in its favour the retention of the MS reading. Translate 'his was a sorrowful heart . . . a double woe: the light of heaven would grow dim for him and he would leave this present (light), the world under the heavens, if he did not reveal the cross'. The subject of *anforlete* is to be understood from *him*; cp Pogatscher, *Anglia* xxiii. 280. For *hador* as a noun see Klaeber, *Beowulf* (1941) 142.

is nu feal[a] siðþan   forð ʒepitenra,
frodra 7 ʒodra   þe us fore pæron
ʒleapra ʒumena;   ic on ʒeoʒoðe pearð
on siðdaʒum   syððan acenned
640 cnihtʒeonʒ hæleð;   ic ne can þæt ic nat
findan on fyrhðe   þæt spa fyrn ʒepearð'.
Elene maðelade   him on andspare,
'Hu is þæt ʒeporden   on þysse perþeode
þæt ʒe spa moniʒfeald   on ʒemynd piton
645 alra tacna ʒehpylc spa Troian[æ]
þurh ʒefeoht fremedon?   Þæt pæs f[ie]r myc[le],
open ealdʒepin   þonne þeos æðele ʒepyrd,
ʒeara ʒonʒum;   ʒe þæt ʒeare cunnon
edre ʒereccan   hpæt þær eallra pæs
650 on manrime   morðorslehtes,   fol. 127ᵇ
dareðlacendra   deadra ʒefeallen
under bordhaʒan;   ʒe þa byrʒenna
under stanhleoðum   7 þa stope spa some
7 þa pinterʒerím   on ʒepritu setton'.
655 Iudas maðelade—   ʒnornsorʒe pæʒ—
'Þe þæs herepeorces,   hlæfdiʒe mín,
for nydþearfe   nean myndʒiaþ
7 þa piʒʒþræce   on ʒepritu setton,
þeoda ʒebæru   7 þis næfre
660 þurh æniʒes mannes   muð ʒehyrdon,
hæleðu[m] cyðan   butan her nuða.'
Him seo æðele cpen   aʒeaf andspare,

(636) *feala*] *feale*. (637) An erasure between *us* and *fore*. (640) Second
ic above the line and a tag. (645) *Troianæ*] *troiana*. (646) *fier mycle*] *fær
mycel*. (661) *hæleðum*] *hæleðu*. (662) Maier read *7spáre*.

(645a) tacna: here 'wonder', 'heroic deed'. Cp Grk. σημεῖον 'sign',
'work of power'.

(645b) For the plural of tribal names in -*æ*, Lat. -*i* see Orosius, ed.
Sweet (EETS 79) 78, 6; 56, 14.

(646b) *mycel* for *mycle* in a comparative construction has been thought
possible; cp *Beo.* 69–70. Such a construction might explain the substitution of *fær* for the necessary comparative. *þonne* can hardly mean 'then'
as suggested by Imelmann in Anglia Beibl xvii. 226; cp, also, Koeppel,
ESt xxx. 376–7. Translate 'that was much longer ago'.

51

'Þiðsæcest ðu to spiðe   soðe 7 rihte
ymb þæt lifes treop   7 nu lytle ær
665 sæʒdest soðlice   be þam siʒebeame
leodum þinum   7 nu on liʒe cyrrest'.
Iudas hire onʒen þinʒode,   cpæð þæt he þæt on ʒehðu
    ʒespræce
7 tpeon spiðost, pende him traʒe hnaʒre.
Him oncpæð hraðe   caseres mæʒ,
670 'Hpæt pe ðæt hyrdon   þurh haliʒe bec
hæleðum cyðan   þæt ahanʒen pæs
on Caluarie   cyninʒes freobearn,
Ʒodes ʒastsunu;   þu scealt ʒeaʒninʒa
pisdom onpreon   spa ʒepritu secʒaþ
675 æfter stedepanʒe,   hpær seo stop sie,
Caluar[i]e   ær þec cpealm nime,
spilt for synnum   þæt ic hie syððan mæʒe
ʒeclænsian   Criste to pillan,
hæleðum to helpe   þæt me haliʒ Ʒod
680 ʒefylle, frea mihtiʒ,   feores inʒeþanc,
peoruda puldorʒeofa,   pillan minne,
ʒasta ʒeocend'.   Hire Iudas oncpæð
stiðhycʒende,   'Ic þa stope ne can
ne þæs panʒes piht   ne þa pisan cann'.
685 Elene maðelode   þurh eorne hyʒe,
'Ic þæt ʒesperiʒe   þurh sunu meotodes,
þone áhanʒnan ʒod   þæt ðu hunʒre scealt
for cneomaʒum   cpylmed peorðan
butan þu forlæte   þa leasunʒa
690 7 me speotollice   soð ʒecyðe'.
Heht þa spa cpicne   corðre lædan,
scufan scyldiʒne—   scealcas ne ʒældon—
in drýʒne seað   þær he duʒuða leas
siomode in sorʒum   seofon nihta fyrst

(671) the first *n* of *ahanʒen* above the line and a tag. (676) *Caluarie*]
caluare.

(668a) Understand the preposition from 'on ʒehðu' or expand 7 to
on as in 311.

695 under hearmlocan hunʒre ʒeþreatod,
clommum beclunʒen 7 þa cleopiʒan onʒan
sarum besylced on þone seofeðan dæʒ,
meðe 7 meteleas— mæʒen pæs ʒespiðrod—
'Ic eop healsie þurh heofona Ӡod
700 þæt ʒe me of ðyssum earfeðum up forlæten,
heanne fram hunʒres ʒeniðlan; ic þæt haliʒe treo
lustum cyðe nu ic hit lenʒ ne mæʒ
helan for hunʒre; is þes hæft to ðan stranʒ, fol. 128ᵃ
þreanyd þæs þearl 7 þes þroht to ðæs heard
705 doʒorrimum; ic adreoʒan ne mæʒ
ne lenʒ helan be ðam lifes treo
þeah ic ær mid dysiʒe þurhdrifen þære
7 ðæt soð to late seolf ʒecneope':—. viiii.

ÞA ðæt ʒehyrde sio þær hæleðum scead,
710 beornes ʒebæro hio bebead hraðe
þæt hine man of nearpe 7 of nydcleofan,
fram þam énʒan hofe up forlete.
Hie ðæt ofstlice efnedon sona
7 hine mid arum up ʒelæddon
715 of carcerne spa him seo cpen bebead.
Stopon þa to þære stope stiðhycʒende
on þa dune úp ðe dryhten ǽr
ahanʒen pæs heofonrices peard,
ʒodbearn on ʒálʒan 7 hpæðre ʒeare nyste,
720 hunʒre ʒehyned hpær sio haliʒ[e] ród
þurh [facen]searu foldan ʒetyned,
lanʒe leʒere fæst, leodum dyrne,
punode pælreste. Þord stunde ahof
elnes oncyðiʒ 7 on Ebrisc spræc,

(715) *bebead* with the prefix above the line and a tag. (716) *stope stið* on an erasure. (718) Erasure after *pæs*. (720) *haliʒe] haliʒ*. (721) *facensearu] searu*.

(717) ðe: 'on which'; cp Kern, ESt li. 12 and lines 162, 416.
(721a) For the emendation see Paris-Psalter lv. 1.
(724a) BT equate with *uncyðiʒ* 'weak', 'ignorant' but the presumable connection with German *Ankündigung*, OE *oncyðan*, makes this unlikely. Translate 'revealing courage', 'bold'. Cp 960.

725 'Dryhten Hælend, þu ðe ahst doma ȝepeald
7 þu ȝeporhtest þurh þines puldres miht
heofon 7 eorðan 7 holmþræce,
sæs sidne fæðm samod ealle ȝesceaft,
7 þu amæte mundum þinum
730 ealne ymbhpyrft 7 úprador
7 þu sylf sitest, siȝora paldend
ofer þam æðelestan enȝelcynne
þe ȝeond lyft fara ð leohte bepundene,
mycle mæȝenþrymme; ne mæȝ þær manna ȝecynd
735 of eorðpeȝum úp ȝeferan
in lichoman mid þa leohtan ȝedryht,
puldres aras; þu ȝeporhtest þa
7 to þeȝnunȝe þinre ȝesettest,
haliȝ 7 heofonlic; þara on hade sint
740 in sindreame syx ȝenemned
þa ymbsealde synt mid syxum eac
fiðrum, ȝefrætpad; fæȝere scínaþ;
þara si[n]t feoper þe on flihte á
þa þeȝnunȝe þrymme bepeotiȝaþ
745 fore onsyne eces deman,
sinȝallice sinȝaþ in puldre
hædrum stefnum heofoncininȝes lof,
poða pliteȝaste 7 þas pord cpeðaþ
clænum stefnum— þam is Ceruphin nama—
750 "Haliȝ is se halȝa heahenȝla Ɉod,
peoroda pealdend; is ðæs puldres ful
heofun 7 eorðe 7 eall heahmæȝen
tire ȝetacnod"; syndon tú on þam,
siȝorcynn on speȝle þe man Seraphin
755 be naman hateð; he sceal Neorxnapanȝ

(731) An erasure (according to Maier on) before *siȝora*. The o of *siȝora*
above the line. (734) *mæȝen þrymme* above the line probably in a later
hand. But cp Sisam, *Studies* 113 (743) *sint*] *sit*.

(739) *þara on hade*: 'in which order'.
(755) Some editors emend 'he sceal' to 'hie sculon' but one angel only
may be intended as Grein-Wülcker (169) suggest. Or *he* is written for
hie whence the singular verb.

7 lifes treo leȝene speorde
haliȝ healdan. Heardecȝ cpacaþ,
beofaþ broȝdenmǽl 7 bleom prixleð
ȝrapum ȝryrefæst; þæs ðu, ꝳod dryhten,
760 pealdest pidan fyrhð 7 þu pomfulle,
scyldpyrcende, sceaðan of radorum
apurpe, ponhydiȝe; þa sio perȝe sceolu
under heolstorhofu hreosan sceolde
in pita forpyrd þær hie in pylme nu
765 dreoȝaþ deaðcpale in dracan fæðme
þeostrum forþylmed. He þinum piðsóc
aldordome; þæs he in ermðum sceal
ealra fula fúl fáh þropian,
þeopned þolian. Þær he þín ne mæȝ
770 pord ápeorpan, is in pitum fæst
ealre synne fruma susle ȝebunden.
ꝳif þin pilla sie, pealdend enȝla,
þæt ricsie se ðe on rode pæs
7 þurh Marian in middanȝeard
775 acenned pearð in cildes had,
þeoden enȝla— ȝif he þin nære,
sunu synna leas næfre he soðra spa feala,
in poruldrice, pundra ȝefremede
doȝorȝerimum no ðu of deaðe hine
780 spa þrymlice, þeoda pealdend,
apeahte for peorodum ȝif he in puldre þin
þurh ða beorhtan bearn ne pære—
ȝedo nu, fæder enȝla, forð beacen þín;
spa ðu ȝehyrdest þone halȝan per,

(757) ecȝ above the line and tag. (767) he may have an accent but
the mark seems to have been incised and has not the usual thickness
at the top. (771) The s of susle has been squeezed between the u and
the l.

(763a) Most editors read heolstorhofu but the metre suggests that
heolstor may be an adjective. Cp, however, PBB x. 481.

(765) dracan fæðme· see Jonah ii, 2.

(768) ealra fula ful: an extension of such phrases as 'eallra þrymma
þrym'. These are probably an imitation of the biblical use of an inten-
sitive genitive. Cp 483.

785 Moyses on meðle   þa ðu, mihta Ʒod,
   Ʒehypdest þam eorle   on þa æðelan tíd
   under beorhhliðe   bán Iosephes
   spa ic þe,   peroda Ƿyn,   Ʒif hit sie pilla þín,
   þurʒ þæt beorhte Ʒesceap   biddan pille
790 þæt me þæt Ʒoldhord   Ʒasta scyppend
   Ʒeopenie   þæt yldum pæs
   lanʒe behyded.   Forlæt nú, lifes Fruma,
   of ðam panʒstede   pynsumne úp,
   under radores ryne,   rec astiʒan
795 lyftlacende;   ic Ʒelyfe þe sel
   7 þy fæstlicor   ferhð staðeliʒe,
   hyht untpeondne   on þone ahanʒnan Crist
   þæt he sie soðlice   sapla nerʒend,
   éce ælmihtiʒ,   Israhela cininʒ,
800 palde pidan ferhð   puldres on heofenum
   á butan ende   ecra Ʒestealda':—

                    .X.

   ÐA of ðære stope   steam úp aras
   spylce réc under radorum.   Þær aræred pearð
   beornes breostsefa;   he mid bæm handum
805 eadiʒ 7 æʒleap   uppeard pleʒade.
   Iudas maþelode   Ʒleap in Ʒeþance,
   'Nu ic þurh soð hafu   seolf Ʒecnapen
   on heardum hiʒe   þæt ðu hælend eart   fol. 129ᵃ
   middanʒeardes; sie ðe mæʒena Ʒod
810 þrymsittendum   þanc butan ende
   þæs ðu me spa meðum   7 spa mánpeorcum

(810) An *m* has been erased after *þrym*.

---

(787) A reference to a Talmudic legend according to which Joseph's
bones, concealed either in the Nile or among the royal tombs, are
miraculously revealed by Moses' prayers. See Emerson, MLN xiv.
331–4.
(805) Judas clapped his hands; cp Junius Psalter xlvi. 1, *plaudite
manibus* 'pleʒiað ʒe mid hondum'. The Latin has *et plauderet ambis
manibus*.

þurh þin puldor inpriӡe   pyrda ӡeryno.
Nu ic þe, bearn Ӡodes,   biddan pille,
peoroda pillӡifa,   nu ic pat þæt ðu eart
815 ӡecyðed 7 acenned   allra cyninӡa þrym
þæt ðu ma ne sie   minra ӡylta
þara þe ic ӡefremede   nalles feam siðum,
metud, ӡemyndiӡ.   Læt mec, mihta Ӡod,
on rimtale   rices þines
820 mid haliӡra   hlyte puniӡan
in þære beorhtan byriӡ,   þær is broðor mín
ӡepeorðod in puldre   þæs he pære pið þec,
Stephanus, heold   þeah he stanӡreopum
porpod pære.   He hafað piӡӡes lean,
825 blæd butan blinne;   sint in bocum his
pundor þa he porhte   on ӡepritum cyðed.'
Onӡan þa pilfæӡen   æfter þam puldres treo
elnes ánhydíӡ   eorðan delfan
under turfhaӡan   þæt he on tpentiӡum
830 fotmælum feor   funde behelede,
under neolum niðer   næsse ӡehydde,
in þeostorcofan—   he ðær þreo mette—
in þam reonian hofe,   roda ætsomne,
ӡreote beӡrauene,   spa hio ӡeardaӡum
835 arleasra sceolu   eorðan beþeahton,
Iudea [cyn];   hie pið Ӡodes bearne
nið áhofun   spa hie no sceoldon
þær hie leahtra fruman   larum ne hyrdon.
Þa pæs modӡemynd   myclum ӡeblissod,
840 hiӡe onhyrded   þurh þæt haliӡe treo,

(836) *cyn* not in MS.

(812b) 'disclose the hidden things of God's Providence'. Cp Timmer, *Neophilologus* xxvi. 24–33; 213–28.
(826b) viz. in Acts.
(827–36) Krapp (*Vercelli Book*) suggests a stop after *þeostorcofan*, and presumably takes *þæt* as relative with antecedent *treo*. But the syntax of *behelede* and *ӡehydde* is then difficult. Holthausen (*Elene* 1936) implies that 827–36 is an anacoluthon, since he puts a dash after *þeostorcofan*. But parenthesis in 832b gives a clearer construction.

inbryrded breostsefa   syððan beacen ʒeseh
haliʒ under hrusan;   he mid handum befenʒ
puldres pynbeam   7 mid peorode áhóf
of foldʒræfe.   Feðeʒestas
845 eodon, æðelinʒas   in on þa ceastre.
Ásetton þa on ʒesyhðe   siʒebeamas þrie
eorlas anhydiʒe   fore Elenan cneo,
collenferhðe;   cpen peorces ʒefeah
on ferhðsefan   7 þa friʒnan onʒan
850 on hpylcum þara beama   bearn pealdendes,
hæleða hyhtʒifa   hanʒen pære,
'Hpæt pe þæt hyrdon   þurh haliʒe bec
tacnum cyðan   þæt tpeʒen mid him
ʒeþropedon   7 he pæs þridda sylf
855 on rode treo;   rodor eal ʒespearc
on þa sliðan tíd;   saʒa ʒif ðu cunne
on hpylcre þyssa þreora   þeoden enʒla,
ʒeþropode,   þrymmes hyrde'.   fol. 129b
Ne meahte hire Iudas—   ne ful ʒere piste—
860 speotole ʒecyþan   be ðam siʒebeame,
on hpylcre se hælend   áhafen pære,
siʒebearn Ʒodes   ær he asettan heht
on þone middel   þære mæran byriʒ
beamas mid bearhtme   7 ʒebidan þær
865 oððæt him ʒecyðde   cyninʒ ælmihtiʒ
pundor for peorodum   be ðam puldres treo.
Ʒesæton siʒerofe,   sanʒ áhofon
rædþeahtende   ymb þa roda þreo
oð þa niʒoðan tíd;   hæfdon neopne ʒefean
870 mærðum ʒemeted;   þa þær meniʒo cpom,
folc unlytel 7 ʒefærenne man
brohton on bære   beorna þreate

(841–2) *seh* above the line and a tag; comma erased after *beacen*;
both *beacen* and first letter of *ʒeseh* on an erasure. (847) The *n* of *cneo*
above the line and a tag.
(855) Three or four letters erased after *rode*.

(861) *hpylcre* may be a mistake for *hpylcne* or due to the poet's
having thought of *rod* rather than *siʒebeam* as the antecedent.

on neapeste— pæs þa niȝoðe tid—
ȝinȝne ȝastleasne. Þa ðær Iudas pæs
875 on modsefan miclum ȝeblissod.
Heht þa asettan saplleasne,
life belidenes lic, on eorðan,
unlifȝendes, 7 up áhof
rihtes pemend þara roda tpa,
880 fyrhðȝleap on fæðme ofer þæt fæȝe hús,
deophycȝende; hit pæs dead spa ær,
lic leȝere fæst, leomu colodon
þreanedum beþeaht; þa sio þridde pæs
áhafen haliȝ; hrá pæs on anbide
885 oððæt him uppan æðelinȝes pæs
ród áræred, rodorcyninȝes beam,
siȝebeacen soð; he sona aras
ȝaste ȝeȝearpod, ȝeador bú samod
lic 7 sapl. Þær pæs lof hafen
890 fæȝer mid þy folce, fæder peorðodon
7 þone soðan, sunu pealdendes
þordum heredon. Sie him puldor 7 þanc
a butan ende eallra
ȝesceafta:—
ÐA pæs þam folce on ferhðsefan
895 inȝemynde— spa him a scyle—
þundor þa þe porhte peoroda dryhten
to feorhnere fira cynne,
lifes lattiop. Þa þær liȝesynniȝ
on lyft astah lacende feond.
900 Onȝan þa hleoðrian helle deofol,
eatol æclæca yfela ȝemyndiȝ,
'Hpæt is þis, la, manna þe minne eft
þurh fyrnȝeflit folȝaþ pyrdeð,

(873) Maier read *tid*. (877) An erasure of four or five letters between
belidenes and *lic*. (878) An erasure between the *n* and *l* of *unlifȝendes*.
(898) *lattiop'*.

(884b) The body was in suspense waiting for the return of the soul.
For the scansion see Das, *op.cit.* 21, 239.

íceð ealdne nið,   æhta strudeð?
905 Þis is sinȝal sacu;   sapla ne moton,
mánfremmende   in minum lenȝ
æhtum puniȝan;   nu cþom elþeodiȝ
þone ic ær on firenum   fæstne talde,
hafað mec bereafod   ríhta ȝehpylces,
910 feohȝestreona;   nis ðæt fæȝer sið.
Feala me se hælend   hearma ȝefremede,
niða nearolicra,   se ðe in Nazareð
afeded pæs;   syððan furþum peox   fol. 130ᵃ
of cildhade   symle cirde to him
915 æhte mine;   ne mot æniȝe nu
rihte spopan;   is his rice brad
ofer middanȝeard,   min is ȝespiðrod,
ræd under roderum;   ic þa rode ne þearf
hleahtre heriȝean;   hpæt, se hælend me
920 in þam enȝan ham   oft ȝetynde
ȝeomrum to sorȝe.   Ic þurh Iudas ær
hyhtful ȝepearð   7 nu ȝehyned eom
ȝóda ȝeasne   þurh Iudas eft,
fáh 7 freondleas;   ȝen ic findan can
925 þúrh þrohtstafaṣ.   piðercyr pið ðan
of ðaṃ pearhtreafum;   ic apecce pið ðe
oðerne cyninȝ   se ehteð þin
7 he forlæteð   lare þine
7 manþeapum   minum folȝaþ
930 ond· þec þonne sendeð   in þa speartestan
7 þa pyrrestan   pitebroȝan
þæt ðu sarum forsoht   piðsæcest fæste
þone ahanȝnan cyninȝ   þam ðu hyrdest ær'.
Him ða ȝleaphydiȝ   Iudas oncpæð,
935 hæleð hildedeor—   him pæs Haliȝ Ȝast
befolen fæste,   fyrhat lufu,

(924) *can*] *ne can.* (926). *apecce*] *æ̆pecce.*

(925b) pið ðan: 'against that'; see Sisam, RES xxii. 267.
(927a) Julian the Apostate under whom Judas is said to have suffered
martyrdom.

peallende ȝepitt,   þurh Þiȝan snyttro—
7 þæt pord ȝecpæð   pisdomes ful,
'Ne þearft ðu spa spiðe   synna ȝemyndiȝ
940 sár nipiȝan   7 sæce ræran,
morðres mánfrea;   þ[ec] se mihtiȝa cyninȝ
in neolnesse   nyðer bescufeð
synpyrcende,   in susla ȝrund,
domes leasne,   se ðe deadra feala
945 porde apehte;   pite ðu þe ȝearpor
þæt ðu unsnyttrum   ánforlete
leohta beorhtost   7 lufan dryhtnes,
þone fæȝran ȝefean   7 on fyrbæðe
suslum beþrunȝen   syððan punodest,
950 ade onæled   7 þær apa scealt,
piðerhycȝende,   perȝðu dreoȝan,
yrmðu butan ende'.   Elene ȝehyrde
hu se feond 7 se freond   ȝeflitu rærdon,
tíreadiȝ 7 traȝ   on tpa halfa,
955 synniȝ 7 ȝesæliȝ;   sefa pæs þe ȝlædra
þæs þe heo ȝehyrde   þone helle sceaþan
oferspiðende,   synna bryttan
7 þa pundrade   ymb þæs peres snyttro,
hu he spa ȝeleafful,   on spa lytlum fæce—
960 7 spa uncyðiȝ—   æfre purde,

941 þec] þæt. (952) An erasure between butan and ende. (954) The l
of halfa above the line. (958) The b of ymb above the line and a tag.

(937b) The Latin has 'Iudas autem fervens in SS., dixit'... The
traditional emendation pitȝan is thus unsuitable. It is tempting to
speculate that piȝa might here be a weak noun from OE pih and thus
'The Holy One'. The existence of the more common homonym piȝa
'warrior' would explain its disuse. Cp Williams, The Conflict of Homonyms
in English.
(941b) See Cosijn, Aanteekeningen op den Beowulf 32.
(957a) Most editors read oferswiðedne (cp VPs 125, 1?). The emendation should probably be accepted.
(960) uncyðiȝ is usually emended to oncyðiȝ (cp unforht in Dream of
the Rood 117). If the prefix is privative or pejorative, the translation may
be 'how he became, in so short a time, and ignorant or wicked as he was,
so full of faith'. For the construction cp 'spa disiȝe' 477; 'spa cpicne' 691
and NED so 14.

ʒleapnesse þurhʒoten;   Ʒode þancode,
puldorcyninʒe þæs hire se pilla ʒelamp
þurh bearn Ʒodes   beʒa ʒehpæðres,
ʒe æt þære ʒesyhðe þæs siʒebeames,
965 ʒe ðæs ʒeleafan þe hio spa leohte oncneop,
puldorfæste ʒife in þæs peres breostum:—

ÐA pæs ʒefreʒe in þære folcsceare,   fol. 130ᵇ
ʒeond þa perþeode   pide læded
mære morʒenspel   maniʒum on andan
970 þara þe dryhtnes á dyrnan poldon,
bod[e]n æfter burʒum   spa brimo fæðm[a]ð
in ceastra ʒehpære   þæt Cristes [rod]
fyrn foldan beʒræfen   funden pære,
selest siʒebeacna   þara þe sið oððe ær,
975 háliʒ under heofenum,   ahafen purde;
ond pæs Iudeum   ʒnornsorʒa mæst,
perum pansæliʒum   pyrda laðost—
þær hie hit for porulde   pendan meahton—
cristenra ʒefean.   Ða sio cpen bebead
980 ofer eorlmæʒen   aras fysan
ricene to rade,   sceoldon Rómparena
ofer heanne holm   hlaford secean
ond þam piʒʒende   pilspella mæst
seolfum ʒesecʒan   þ[æt]ðæt siʒorbeacen
985 þurh meotodes est   meted pære,
funden in foldan   þæt ær feala mæla
behyded pæs halʒum to teonan,
cristenum folce;   þa ðam cininʒe pearð
þurh þa mæran pord   mód ʒeblissod,
990 ferhð ʒefeonde;   næs þa fricʒendra

(971) *boden*] *bodan. fæðmað*] *fæðmeð*. (972) *rod* not in the MS. (974)
siʒe becna with *a* above the line and a tag. (984) *þæt*] *þe*. (989) Maier
read *mód* but the mark is apparently the tail of the letter above.

(974–5) Note the sg. verb after 'þara þe'; cp 970, 1288; Grossmann,
Das ags. Relativ 56–61; Bauch, *op.cit.* 54–7.

(978) Possibly 'if only they could alter it!' Cp Cosijn, *Aanteekeningen
op den Beowulf* 32. Or read *þæt . . . ne meahton* as suggested by Grein.

under ȝoldhoman   ȝád in burȝum,
feorran ȝeferede;   pæs him frofra mæst,
ȝeporden in porlde   æt ðam pillspelle,
hlihende hyȝe,   þe him hereræspan
995 ofer eastpeȝas,   aras brohton
hu ȝesundne sið   ofer s[p]onrade
secȝas mid siȝecpen   asete[d] hæfdon
on Creca land;   hie se casere heht
ofstum myclum   eft ȝearpian
1000 sylfe to siðe;   secȝas ne ȝældon
syððan andspare   edre ȝehyrdon,
æðelinȝes pord.   Heht he Elenan hǽl
abeodan, beadurofre   ȝif hie brim nesen,
7 ȝesundne sið   settan mosten,
1005 hæleð hpætmode   to þære halȝan byriȝ.
Heht hire þa aras   eac ȝebeodan,
Constantinus   þæt hio cirican þær
on þam beorhhliðe   beȝra rædum
ȝetimbrede,   tempel dryhtnes
1010 on Caluarie   Criste to pillan,
hæleðum to helpe   þær sio haliȝe ród
ȝemeted pæs,   mærost beama
þara þe ȝefruȝnen   foldbuende
on eorðpeȝe;   hio ȝeefnde spa
1015 siððan pinemaȝas   pestan brohton
ofer laȝufæsten   leofspell maniȝ.
Ða seo cpen bebead   cræftum ȝetyde
sundor asecean,   þa selestan,
þa þe prætlicost   pyrcan cuðon
1020 stanȝefoȝum,   on þam stedepanȝe
ȝirpan Ᵹodes tempel   spa hire ȝasta peard
reord of roderum;   heo þa rode heht
ȝolde bepeorcean   7 ȝimcynnum,   fol. 131ᵃ
mid þam æðelestum   eorcnanstanum,

(996) *sponrade*] *spon rade*. (997) *aseted*] *aseten*. (1019) The *n* of *cuðon* above the line and a tag.

(1003b) nesen: for the pret. subj. see Prollius, *op.cit.* 19.

1025 besett[a]n searocræftum   7 þa in seolfren fæt
     locum belucan   þær þæt lifes treo,
     selest siȝebeama   siððan punode
     æðel[e], [u]nbrȩce;   þær bið a ȝearu
     praðu pannhalum   pita ȝehpylces,
1030 sæce 7 sorȝe;   hie sona þær
     þurh þa halȝan ȝesceaft   helpe findaþ,
     ȝodcunde ȝife.   Spylce Iudas onfenȝ
     æfter fyrstmearce   fulpihtes bæð
     7 ȝeclænsod pearð   Criste ȝetrype,
1035 lifpearde leof;   his ȝeleafa pearð
     fæst on ferhðe   siððan frofre ȝast
     píc ȝepunode   in þæs peres breostum,
     bylde to bote;   he þæt betere ȝeceas,
     puldres pynne   7 þam pyrsan piðsóc,
1040 deofulȝildum   7 ȝedpolan fylde,
     unrihte ǽ;   him pearð ece cyninȝ,
     meotud milde, Ʒod,   mihta pealdend:—

                    . xiii .

     ÞA pæs ȝefulpad   se ðe ær feala tida
     leoht ȝearu...
1045 inbryrded breostsefa   on þæt betere lif,
     ȝepended to puldre.   Huru pyrd ȝescreaf
     þæt he spa ȝeleaffull   7 spa leof Ʒode
     in porldrice   peorðan sceolde
     Criste ȝecpeme.   þæt ȝecyðed pearð
1050 siððan Elene heht   Eusebium
     on rædȝeþeaht,   Rome bisceop
     ȝefetian on fultum,   forðsnoterne,

(1025) *besettan*] *Be setton.* (1028) *æðele unbrȩce*] *æðelu anbrȩce.* (1041)
cyning] *rex.*

(1028a) For the emendation cp *J J J* 23. *æðele* is required by the masculine antecedent *siȝebeam.* The final *u* of the MS reading may be due to
anticipation but see note to 861. The MS *anbrȩce* is for *unbrȩce* 'inviolable'; it may be a scribal error or contain the negative *on-.* For half-
lines made up of two adjectives see Klaeber, *Anglia* xxviii. 440.

hæleða ȝerædum   to þære halȝan byriȝ
þæt he ȝesette   on sacerdhád,
1055 in Ierusalem,   Iudas þam folce
to bisceope,   burȝum on innan,
þurh Ȝastes ȝife   to Ȝodes temple,
cræftum ȝecorene,   7 hine Cyriacus
þurh snyttro ȝeþeaht   syððan nemde
1060 nipan stefne;   nama pæs ȝecyrred
beornes in burȝum   on þæt betere forð,
'ǽ hælendes'.   þa ȝen Elenan pæs
mód ȝemynde   ýmb þa mæran pyrd
ȝeneahhe for þam næȝlum   þe ðæs nerȝendes
1065 fét þurhpodon   7 his folme spa some,
mid þam on rode pæs   rodera pealdend
ȝefæstnod, frea mihtiȝ;   be ðam friȝnan onȝan
Cristenra cpen,   Cyriacus bæd
þæt hire þa ȝina   ȝastes mihtum
1070 ymb pundorpyrd   pillan ȝefylde,
onpriȝe puldorȝifum   7 þæt pord ácpæð,
to þam bisceope   bald reordode,
'þu me, eorla hleo,   þone æðelan beam,
róde rodercininȝ[es]   ryhte ȝetæhtesð   fol. 131ᵇ
1075 on þa áhanȝen pæs   hæðenum folmum
ȝasta ȝeocend,   Ȝodes aȝen bearn,
neriȝend fira;   mec þæra næȝla ȝén
on fyrhðsefan   fyrpet mynȝaþ;
polde ic þæt ðu funde   þa ðe in foldan ȝén
1080 deope bedolfen   dierne sindon,
heolstre behyded;   á min hiȝe sorȝað,
reoniȝ reoteð   7 ȝeresteð no
ærþan me ȝefylle   fæder ælmihtiȝ,
pereda pealdend,   pillan minne,
1085 niða nerȝend   þurh þara næȝla cyme

(1074) rodercininȝes] rodera cininȝ/. Cp PBB x. 518.

_____

(1053) For ȝerædum see JJJ 39–40.
(1074a) The erroneous assumption that 'eorla hleo' referred to God
may have given rise to the corruption in the text. The phrase would
then be parallel to 'rodera cininȝ'. _Róde_ should perhaps be omitted.

65

haliȝ of hiehða. Nu ðu hrædlice
eallum eaðmedum, ar selesta,
þine bene onsend in ða beorhtan ȝesceaft,
on puldres pyn, bide piȝena þrym
1090 þæt þe ȝecyðe cyninȝ ælmihtiȝ
hord under hrusan þæt ȝehyded ȝén
duȝuðum dyrne deoȝol bideð'.
þa se halȝa onȝan hyȝe staðolian,
breostum onbryrded bisceop þæs folces,
1095 ȝlædmód eode ȝumena þreate
Ᵹod herȝendra, 7 þa ȝeornlice
Cyriacus on Caluariȩ
hleor onhylde, hyȝerune ne mað,
Ᵹastes mihtum to Ᵹode cleopode
1100 eallum eaðmedum, bæd him enȝla peard
ȝeopeniȝean uncuðe pyrd
nipan on nearpe hpær he þara næȝla spiðost
on þam panȝstede penan þorfte.
Leort ða tacen forð þær hie to sæȝon
1105 fæder, frofre ȝast, ðurh fyres bleo
up eðiȝean þær þa æðelestan
hæleða ȝerædum hydde pæron,
þurh nearusearpe, næȝlas on eorðan.
Ða cpom semninȝa sunnan beorhtra
1110 lacende liȝ; leode ȝesapon
hira pillȝifan pundor cyðan
ða ðær of heolstre spylce heofonsteorran
oððe ȝodȝimmas ȝrunde ȝetenȝe,
næȝlas of nearpe neoðan scinende
1115 leohte lixton; leode ȝefæȝon,
peorud pillhreðiȝ, sæȝdon puldor Ᵹode

(1104) A capital L erased before *Leort*. (1116) A mark over the *r* of *hreðig* but it differs in shape from the usual accent.

(1106a) Sievers, *Anglia* i. 578 read *siðiȝean* but the MS reading makes passable sense.

(1113a) Many editors emend to *ȝoldȝimmas* on account of Latin 'tamquam aurum fulgens in terra'. But *ȝodȝimmas* 'divine jewels', 'heavenly bodies' (cp Tolkien, *Medium Aevum* iii. 104–5) is in keeping with *heofonsteorran* in 1112.

ealle ánmode þeah hie ær pæron
þurh deofles spild   in ӡedpolan lanӡe,
acyrred fram Criste;   hie cpædon þus,
1120 'Nu þe seolfe ӡeseoð   siӡores tacen,
soðpundor ᴣodes   þeah þe piðsocun ǽr
mid leasinӡum.   Nu is in leoht cymen,
onpriӡen pyrda biӡanӡ;   puldor þæs aӡe
on heannesse   heofonrices ᴣod.'
1125 Ða þæs ӡeblissod   se ðe to bote ӡehþearf
þurh bearn ᴣodes,   bisceop þara leoda
nipan stefne;   he þan næӡlan onfenӡ
eӡesan ӡeáclod   7 þære arpyrðan
cpene brohte;   hæfde Ciriacus
1130 eall ӡefylled   spa him seo æðele bebead,
pifes pillan;   þa þæs popes hrinӡ,
hat heafodpylm,   ofer hleor ӡoten;
nalles for torne   tearas feollon
ofer þira ӡespon;   puldre [i]s ӡefylled
1135 cpene pilla;   heo on cneop sette
leohte ӡeleafan,   lác peorðode
blissum hremiӡ   þe hire brunӡen þæs
ӡnyrna to ӡeoce;   ᴣode þancode,   fol. 132ᵃ

(1120) The last two letters of *seolfe* on an erasure. (1134) *puldre is*]
puldres.

(1131b) Cp *Guth.* 1339; *Crist* 537; *Andreas* 1278. Some editors have
supposed that the kenning meant 'globe of weeping', 'tear'; cp Kock,
JJJ 5-6; *Anglia* xliv. 106. This view has in its favour the apparent
parallelism of 'hat heafodpylm'. But it may mean 'circle (eye socket)
of weeping', when the conception is of hot tears overflowing like water
boiling over from a cauldron. *E(a)ӡhrinӡ* 'eye-socket' might suggest
such a kenning; cp Brooks, *English and Germanic Studies* ii. 68–74.

(1134a) þira ӡespon: 'web of wires or filigree work'. Perhaps, as the
tears fell over St Helena's breast, a pendant ornamented with filigree
or gold thread. Cp *hrinӡa ӡespon* (MS *ӡesponӡ*) Gen. 377.

(1134b) If *þæs* is understood from 1131, *puldres* is either an unrecorded
adverb 'gloriously' or genitive after *ӡefylled*, 'fulfilled with glory'. Or
puldres could be a corruption of *puldr is*; cp *moncyn is=moncynnes*,
in Rypins, *Three Old English Prose Texts* (EETS 161) 67, 16; or, as we
have assumed, of *puldre is*; cp the parallel construction in 452. Translate 'the queen's will is fulfilled gloriously'.

    siȝora dryhtne   þæs þe hio soð ȝecneop
1140 andpeardlice   þæt pæs oft bodod
    feor ær beforan   fram fruman porulde
    folcum to frofre;   heo ȝefylled pæs
    pisdomes ȝife   7 þa pic beheold
    haliȝ heofonlic ȝast,   hreðer peardode,
1145 æðelne innoð;   spa hie ælmihtiȝ,
    siȝebearn Ꝺodes,   sioððan freoðode:7

.xiiii.

    ONȝan þa ȝeornlice   ȝastȝerynum
    on sefan secean soðfæstnesse,
    peȝ to puldre;   huru peorda Ꝺod
1150 ȝefullæste,   fæder on roderum,
    cininȝ ælmihtiȝ,   þæt seo cpen beȝeat
    pillan in porulde;   pæs se pitedóm
    þurh fyrnpitan   beforan sunȝen
    eall æfter orde   spa hit eft ȝelamp
1155 ðinȝa ȝehpylces;   þeodcpen onȝan
    þurh Ꝺastes ȝife   ȝeorne secan,
    nearpe ȝeneahhe   to hpan hio þa næȝlas selost
    7 deorlicost   ȝedon meahte
    duȝoðum to hroðer,   hpæt þæs pære dryhtnes pilla.
1160 Heht ða ȝefetiȝean   forðsnotterne
    ricene to rune,   þone þe rædȝeþeaht
    þurh ȝleape miht   ȝeorne cuðe,
    frodne on ferhðe   7 hine friȝnan onȝan
    hpæt him þæs on sefan   selost þuhte
1165 to ȝelæstenne   7 his lare ȝeceas
    þurh þeodscipe;   he hire [þriste] oncpæð,
    'Þæt is ȝedafenlic   þæt ðu dryhtnes pord
    on hyȝe healde,   haliȝe rune,
    cpen selest[e],   7 þæs cininȝes bebod

(1166) *þriste* not in MS. (1169) *seleste*] *selest.*

(1149b) Editors read *we(o)ro/uda* but cp Sievers-Brunner §159 n. 8.

1170 ȝeorne beȝanȝe   nu þe Ʒod sealde
saple siȝesped   7 snyttro cræft,
neriȝend fira;   þu ðas næȝlas hat
þam æðelestan   eorðcyninȝa,
burȝaȝendra,   on his bridels dón
1175 meare to midlum;   þæt maniȝum sceall
ȝeond middanȝeard   mære peorðan
þonne æt sæcce mid þy   oferspiðan mæȝe
feonda ȝehpylcne   þonne fyrdhpate
on tpa healfe   tohtan secaþ,
1180 speordȝeniðlan   þær hie [siȝor] pillað,
prað við praðum.   He ah æt piȝȝe sped,
siȝor æt sæcce   7 sybbe ȝehpær,
æt ȝefeohte frið   se ðe fo[r]an lædeð
bridels on blancan   þonne beadurofe
1185 æt ȝárþræce,   ȝuman ȝecoste
berað bord 7 ord;   þis bið beorna ȝehpam
við æȝlæce   unoferspiðed
pæpen æt piȝȝe   be ðam se pitȝa sanȝ
snottor searuþancum—   sefa deop ȝepód,
1190 pisdomes ȝepitt—   he þæt pord ȝecpæð,
"Cuþ þæt ȝepyrðeð   þæt þæs cyninȝes sceal
mearh under modeȝum   midlum ȝepeorðod,
bridelshrinȝum;   bið þæt beacen Ʒode
haliȝ nemned   7 se hpæteadiȝ
1195 piȝȝe peorðod   se þæt picȝ byr[e]ð" '.
þa þæt ofstlice   eall ȝelæste   fol. 132ᵇ
Elene for eorlum,   æðelinȝes heht,

(1180) *sigor*] *ymb*. (1183) *foran*] *fonan*. (1189) A letter erased after *deop*. (1195) *byreð*] *byrð*.

(1177) A subj. after *þonne* is unusual but here may indicate the subjective content of the clause; see Prollius, *Über den syntact. Gebrauch des Conjunctivs* 27.

(1180) The MS reading *ymb* may conceal a word with an initial *s* such as *sinc*; cp *Beowulf* 1204. Many editors read *ymb siȝe (siȝor) pinnað*.

(1188b) Zechariah xiv, 20.

(1195b) Note *se* for *þone*; cp *Genesis* 2119; Grossmann, *op.cit.* 34. The metre requires *byreð*.

beorna beaȝȝifan, bridels frætpan,
hire selfre suna sende to lace
1200 ofer ȝeofenes stream ȝife unscynde.
Heht þa tosomne þa heo seleste
mid Iudeum ȝumena piste,
hæleða cynnes, to þære halȝan byriȝ
cuman in þa ceastre; þa seo cpen onȝan
1205 læran leofra heap þæt hie lufan dryhtnes
7 sybbe spa same sylfra betpeonum,
freondræddenne fæste ȝelæston,
leahtorlease in hira lifes tíd
ond þæs latteopes larum hyrdon
1210 cristenum þeapum þe him Cyriacus
bude, boca ȝleap; þæs se bissceophad
fæȝere befæsted; oft him feorran to
laman, limseoce, lefe cpomon,
healte, heorudreoriȝe, hreofe 7 blinde,
1215 heane, hyȝeȝeomre; symle hælo þær
æt þam bisceope, bote fundon,
ece to aldre. Ða ȝén him Elene forȝeaf
sincpeorðunȝa þa hio þæs siðes fus
eft to eðle 7 þa eallum bebead
1220 on þam ȝumrice Ȝod herȝendum,
perum 7 pifum, þæt hie peorðeden
mode 7 mæȝene þone mæran dæȝ,
heortan ȝehiȝdum, in ðam sio haliȝe ród
ȝemeted þæs, mærost beama
1225 þara þe of eorðan up ápeoxe,
ȝeloden under leafum; þæs þa lencten aȝan
butan syx nihtum ær sumeres cyme
on Mai[u]s monað; sie þara manna ȝehpam
behliden helle duru, heofones ontyned,

(1228) *Maius monað*] *maias.kl*..

(1228a) The abbreviation must be expanded to *kalend* 'month' not *kalendas* as *Maias* suggests. The kalends of May fall in the second half of April and the reading *kalendas* is, therefore, appropriate neither for the festival of the Invention on May 3, nor for the beginning of summer on May 9. For the reading in the text see Sisam, *Studies* 14.

1230 ece ʒeopenad   enʒla rice,
      dream unhpilen   7 hira dæl scired
      mid Marian   þe on ʒemynd nime
      þære deorestan   dæʒpeorðunʒa,
      rode under roderum   þa se ricesða,
1235 ealles oferpealdend,   earme beþeahte. finit:—

                          .xv.

      ÞUS ic fród 7 fús,   þurh þæt fæcne hus,
      pordcræft pæf   7 pundrum læs,
      þraʒum þreodude   7 ʒeþanc reodode,
      nihtes nearpe;   nysse ic ʒearpe,
1240 be ðære [rode] riht   ær me rumran ʒeþeaht,
      þurh ða mæran miht,   on modes þeaht,
      pisdóm onpreah;   ic pæs peorcum fáh,
      synnum asæled,   sorʒum ʒepæled,
      bitrum ʒebunden,   bisʒum beþrunʒen,
1245 ær me lare onlaʒ   þurh leohtne had,

(1240) *rode* not in MS. (1241) The *þ* of *þeaht* added later. (1244)
bisʒum] *besʒum* with an *i* added above the line.

(1232) For the subjunctive cp Prollius, *op.cit.* 11.
(1236b) Cp 88o. *Hus* is a metaphor for the poet's body comparable to
feorʒbold, feorhhus. Fæcne either means 'deceitful' or is an example of the
otherwise unique sense 'old'. See BTS, s.v. *fæcne. þurh* means either
'because of' or 'by means of'.
(1237a) K. Brooks reads *wordcræft awæf* (*Medium Aevum* xxviii. 110).
(1238b) The rhyme supports the unique *reodode.* The supposition
that it is a variant of *hridian* 'sift' is supported by the use of a similar
metaphor in Otfrid (*Evangelienbuch* iv. 13, 16), where it expresses the
sifting image of Luke xxii, 31: 'thaz muast er redan iu thaz muat, so
man korn in sibe duat': see Grein-Köhler, s.v. *reodian.* The absence of
the second *r* may be due either to the influence of *hriðian* or to the
rhyme.
(1240a) Grein's emendation.
(1243a) The image is from Proverbs v, 22. Cp Menner, *Sol. & Sat.*
132–3.
(1244a) The rhyme supports the hapax *bitrum*; cp Klaeber, ESt lv.
284; Ekwall, Anglia Beibl xxxiii. 65.
(1245b) 'gloriously'; cp *Beo.* 1335.

ȝamelum to ȝeoce, ȝife unscynde
mæȝencyninȝ ámæt 7 on ȝemynd beȝeat,
torht ontynde, tidum ȝerymde,
báncofan onband, breostlocan onpand,
1250 leoðucræft onleac þæs ic lustum breac,
pillum in porlde; ic þæs puldres treopes
oft nales æne hæfde inȝemynd
ær ic þæt pundor onpriȝen hæfde,   fol. 133ᵃ
ymb þone beorhtan beam spa ic on bocum fand,
1255 pyrda ȝanȝum, on ȝepritum cyðan
be ðam siȝebeacne. A pæs sæc[ȝ] oð ðæt
cnysseð cearpelmum, ᚻ. drusende
þeah he in medohealle maðmas þeȝe,
æplede ȝold . ᛗ. ȝnornode,

(1256) sæcȝ] sæcc.

(1247b) The rhyme suggests that beȝeat is from beȝietan but deriva-
tion from beȝeotan makes better sense.

(1249) Cp 86b. (1250) Cp 522.

(1256b) Most editors read secȝ. For sæcȝ see Introduction p. 12; but
sæcc may be for sec; cp Andreas 1225; Waldere 1. 5; Beo. 2863.

(1257b) The c-rune usually stands for cen 'torch'; see Rune Poem
16–18. 'Cen drusende' would mean 'dying torch'. There is a comparable
image in Bibliothek der ags. Prosa iii. 148: 'Spa hpilc man spa sæȝð
leasunȝa on his nehstan, his leohtfet bið acpænced on ðam ytemestan
dæȝe'. In both passages the life of man is compared to a torch or lamp.
The interpretation cyn (Trautmann, BB i. 70) and also cene (Kemble
Archaeologia xxviii, 363) have been supported by reference to Crist 797,
but although the partial spellings in Riddle 65 might be compared it is
more probabᴌe that in Crist the first three runes together spell cyn
'mankind'. Cp Riddle 20. But some support for the interpretation cene
might be seen in the spelling coen in St John's College 17 and in the
Welsh gloss guichr 'anger', 'impetuous' in MS Bodley Auct. F. 4. 32
(cp Derolez p. 159). Or cen might have been taken to equal cyn as wen
equals wyn.

(1259a) Usually interpreted 'embossed gold', since æppel means any
spherical object, such as an eyeball, as well as 'apple'. Embossed gold
would presumably refer to objects with embossed work such as can be
seen on the Sutton Hoo helmet. Cp R. Woolf, Juliana p. 87. But ON
apalgrár, Germ. apfelgrau etc (cp NED Dapple-grey) suggest that
æpled might mean 'circular' as well as 'spherical'. The semantic development seems to have occurred, also, in French gris-pommelé. 'The

1260 ·ᛉ· ȝefera nearusorȝe dreah,
enȝe rune þær him. ᛗ. fore
milpaðas mæt, modiȝ þræȝde,
pirum ȝeplenced. ᚦ . is ȝespiðrad,
ȝomen æfter ȝearum, ȝeoȝoð is ȝecyrred,
1265 ald onmedla. ᚾ . pæs ȝeara
ȝeoȝoðhades ȝlæm; nu synt ȝeardaȝas
æfter fyrstmearce forð ȝepitene,
lífpynne ȝeliden spa.ᛚ.toȝlideð,

(1263) The p-rune has been written twice and the first one erased.
(1268) An erasure before the l-rune.

---

rounded gold' may have been used in contrast with the 'twisted gold'
either to mean coins, such as the *solidi* which were common in the
Islands of Bornholm, Öland and Götland, Zealand and Funen during
the Migration Period; or the phrase might refer to some circular object
such as a ring, armlet or torque, or an annular or saucer brooch, or to
the bars of gold which were made into rings and used like the 'twisted
gold' as currency. Cp Shetelig and Falk, *Scandinavian Archaeology*,
trans. E. V. Gordon, 230 f. The y-rune is usually *yr* 'bow'; see *Rune
Poem* 84–6. But it may, also, be 'horn' as suggested by Holthausen in
Anglia xxxv. 175–7 which would fit well in *Fates* 103. For the view
that the runes are only names see Sisam, *Studies* 21–8; cp Elliott, *English
Studies* xxxiv. 53.

(1260a) 'an inevitable companion'; cp Bede's *Death Song neidfaeru*
'inevitable journey'. The n-rune stands for *nyd* 'necessity'.

(1261a) Perhaps a pun: 'oppressive secret' and 'narrow rune'.

(1261b) The e-rune stands for *eoh* 'horse'.

(1263b) The p-rune stands for *pyn* 'joy'; cp Sievers, *Anglia* xiii. 3–4.

(1265b) The u-rune usually stands for *ur* 'aurochs', 'bison'; see *Rune
Poem* 4–6. Kemble, *op.cit.* 363, suggested *ur* 'of old'; Cosijn, *Verslagen en
Mededeelingen der Konink. Akademie van Wetenschappen van Amsterdam*
(Afd. Letterkunde 3rd ser.) vii. 56–7, Gollancz, *Cynewulf's Christ* 181–2,
Sisam, *op.cit.* 27, all suggest *ur(e)* 'our'. This has been supported by the
gloss *noster* in Cott. Dom. A ix but the Latin glosses in this MS are
probably the work of an Elizabethan antiquary; see Hempl, MPh i.
135–41; Sisam, *op.cit.* 18. The context and parallelism require a meaning
'wealth' perhaps related to Latin *aurum* PG. *urom as suggested by
Sievers (*Anglia* xiii. 7); cp Norwegian *Rune Poem* 2–3 for *ur* 'dross'. Or
ur 'bison' might have been thought to have the double sense of *feoh*.
This interpretation has at least the advantage of fitting *Fates* 101 and
Crist 805, also.

(1268b) The l-rune is *lagu* 'water' Cp *swa lagu toglideþ*, Vercelli
Homily X f. 70.

flodas ʒefysde.　. æʒhpam bið
1270　læne under lyfte;　landes frætpe
ʒepitaþ under polcnum　pinde ʒeliccost
þonne he for hæleðum　hlud astiʒeð,
pæðeð be polcnum,　pedende færeð,
7 eft semninʒa　spiʒe ʒepyrðeð
1275　in nedcleofan　nearpe ʒeheaðrod,
þream forþrycced;　spa þeos por[u]ld
eall ʒepiteð
7 eac spa some　þe hire on purdon
atydrede　tionleʒ nimeð,
1280　ðonne Dryhten sylf　dom ʒeseceð
enʒla peorude;　sceall æʒhpylc ðær
reordberendra　riht ʒehyran
dæda ʒehpylcra　þurh þæs Deman muð
7 porda spa same,　ped ʒesyllan
1285　eallra unsnyttro　ær ʒesprecenra,
þristra ʒeþonca.　þonne on þreo dæleð
in fyres fenʒ　folc anra ʒehpylc
þara þe ʒepurdon　on pidan feore
ofer sidne ʒrund;　soðfæste bioð
1290　yfemest in þam ade,　eadiʒra ʒedryht,
duʒuð domʒeorne;　spa hie adreoʒan maʒon
7 butan earfeðum　eaðe ʒeþolian,
modiʒra mæʒen.　Him ʒemetʒaþ eall
e[lð]es leoma　spa him eðost bið,
1295　sylfum ʒeseftost;　synfulle beoð
mane ʒemenʒde,　in ðam midle þread,
hæleð hiʒeʒeomre,　in hatne pylm,
þrosme beþehte.　Bið se þridda dæl,
apyrʒede pomsceaðan,　in þæs pylmes ʒrund,
1300　lease leodhatan,　liʒe befæsted,
þurh ærʒepyrht,　arleasra sceolu,

(1276) *poruld*] *porld*. (1294) *eldes*] *eðles*.

(1269b) The f-rune is *feoh* 'property'.
(1276b) For the emendation cp *Phoenix* 501.
(1294a) Zupitza reads *eldes*; Holthausen *ældes*. Cp Introduction p. 12.

in ʒleda ʒripe.   Ɉode no syððan
of ðam morðorhofe   in ʒemynd cumað,
puldorcyninʒe   ac hie porpene beoð
1305 of ðam heaðupylme   in helle ʒrund,
tornʒeniðlan.   Bið þam tpam dælum
unʒelice;   moton enʒla frean
ʒeseon, siʒora ʒod;   hie asodene beoð,
asundrod fram synnum   spa smæte ʒold
1310 þæt in pylme bið   pomma ʒehpylces,
þurh ofnes fýr,   eall ʒeclænsod,
amered 7 ʒemylted;   spa bið þara manna ælc fol. 133ᵇ
ascyred 7 asceaden   scylda ʒehpylcre,
deopra firena,   þurh þæs domes fýr.
1315 Moton þonne siðþan   sybbe brucan,
eces eadpelan;   him bið enʒla peard
milde 7 bliðe   þæs ðe hie mána ʒehpylc
forsapon, synna peorc   7 to suna metudes
pordum cleopodon;   forðan hie nu on plite scinaþ
1320 enʒlum ʒelice,   yrfes brucaþ,
puldorcyninʒes   to pidan feore.   aMeN:—

(1309b) Cp Proverbs xvii, 3. The image is a commonplace in patristic writings.

75

BIBLIOGRAPHY

Compiled by M.J. Swanton

MANUSCRIPT

AVONTO, L., *L'Ospedale di S. Brigida degli Scoti e il 'Vercelli Book'*, Vercelli, 1973.

BORGOGNONE, F., *Problema del Vercelli Book*, Alessandria, 1951.

COOK, A.S., *Cardinal Guala and the Vercelli Book*, Sacramento, 1888.

DEROLEZ, R., *Runica Manuscripta: the English Tradition*, Bruges, 1954, pp. 391–96.

FELL, C.E., 'Richard Cleasby's notes on the Vercelli Codex', *Leeds Studies in English*, NS, xii (1981), 13–42; xv (1984), 1–19.

FÖRSTER, M., *Il Codice Vercellese con Omelie e Poesie in Lingua Anglosassone*, Rome, 1913.

——'Der Vercelli-Codex CXVII nebst Abdruck einiger altenglischer Homilien der Handschrift', *Festschrift für Lorenz Morsbach*, Halle, 1913, pp. 20–179.

HALSALL, M., 'Vercelli and the Vercelli Book', *PMLA*, lxxxiv (1969), 1545–50.

——'Benjamin Thorpe and the Vercelli Book', *English Language Notes*, vi (1969), 164–69.

——'More about C. Maier's transcript of the Vercelli Book', *English Language Notes*, viii (1970), 3–6.

HERBEN, S.J., 'The Vercelli Book: a new hypothesis', *Speculum*, x (1935), 91–94.

KELLER, W., *Angelsächsische Palaeographie*, Berlin, 1906.

KER, N.R., 'C. Maier's transcript of the Vercelli Book', *Medium Ævum*, xix (1950), 17–25.

——*Catalogue of Manuscripts containing Anglo-Saxon*, Oxford, 1957.

MAIER, C., *Beschreibung des Codex Capitulare Vercellensis, n. CXVII* (1834). Lincoln's Inn MS. Misc. 312.

MARTIN, M., 'A note on marginalia in the Vercelli Book', *Notes and Queries*, ccxxiii (1978), 485–86.

77

RICCI, A., 'Il codice Anglossassone di Vercelli nel primo centenario della sua scoperta', *Rivista delle Biblioteche e degli Archivi*, xxxiii (1923), 13–19.

SCRAGG, D.G., 'Accent marks in the Old English Vercelli Book', *NM*, lxxii (1971), 699–710.

——'The compilation of the Vercelli Book', *Anglo-Saxon England*, ii (1973), 189–207; reprinted in M.P. RICHARDS, ed., *Anglo-Saxon Manuscripts: Basic Readings*, New York (1994), pp. 317–43.

SISAM, C., *The Vercelli Book*. Early English Manuscripts in Facsimile, xix, Copenhagen, 1976.

SISAM, K., 'Marginalia in the Vercelli Book', *Studies*, pp. 109–18.

SZARMACH, P.E., 'The Scribe of the Vercelli Book', *Studia Neophilologica*, li (1979), 179–88.

TEMPLE, E., *Anglo-Saxon Manuscripts 900–1066*, London, 1976.

WÜLCKER, R.P., *Codex Vercellensis. Die angelsæchsische Handschrift zu Vercelli in getreuer Nachbildung*, Leipzig, 1894.

EDITIONS

COOK, A.S., *The Old English Elene, Phoenix, and Physiologus*, New Haven, Connecticut (1919).

ETTMÜLLER, L., *Engla and Seaxna Scôpas and Bôceras*, Quedlinburg (1850), lines 1–193 and 1236–621.

GREIN, C.W.M., *Bibliothek der ags Poesie*, II, Göttingen (1858); revised R.P. WÜLKER, Leipzig (1894).

GRIMM, J., *Andreas und Elene*, Cassel (1840).

HOLTHAUSEN, F., *Cynewulfs Elene*, Heidelberg (1905).

KEMBLE, J.M., *The Poetry of the Codex Vercellensis*, II, London (1856).

KENT, C.W., *Elene: an Old English Poem*, Boston, Massachussets (1889).

KÖRNER, K., *Einleitung in das Studium des Angelsächsischen*, II, Heilbronn (1880) lines 1–275.

KRAPP, G.P., *The Vercelli Book*, Anglo-Saxon Poetic Records II, New York (1932).

LUPI, S., *Cynewulf, Sant'Elena*, Naples (1951).

NELSON, M., *Judith, Juliana, and Elene: Three Fighting Saints*, New York (1991).

THORPE, B., Appendix B in C.P. COOPER *Report on Rymer's Foedera*, London (1836).

ZUPITZA, J., *Cynewulfs Elene*, Berlin (1877).

BIBLIOGRAPHY

TRANSLATIONS

BRADLEY, S.A.J., *Anglo-Saxon Poetry*, London (1982).

GARNETT, J.M., *Elene; Judith; Athelstan, or the Fight at Brunanburh; and Byrhtnoth, or the Fight at Maldon*, Boston, Massachussets (1889).

GORDON, R.K., *Anglo-Saxon Poetry*, London (1927); revised edition 1954.

GREIN, C.W.M., *Dichtungen der Angelsachsen stabreimend übersetzt*, II, Göttingen (1859).

HOLT, L.H., *The Elene of Cynewulf*, New York (1904).

KEMBLE, J.M., *The Poetry of the Codex Vercellensis*, II, London (1856).

KENNEDY, C.W., *The Poems of Cynewulf*, London (1910).

MENZIES, J., *Cynewulf's Elene, A Metrical Translation*, Edinburgh (1895).

NELSON, M., *Judith, Juliana, and Elene: Three Fighting Saints*, New York (1991).

OLIVERO, F., *Traduzioni dalla poesia Anglo-sassone*, Bari (1915), lines 99–147, 219–60, 725–801.

WEYMOUTH, R.F., *A Literal Translation of Cynwulf's Elene*, London (1888).

BACKGROUND

BODDEN, M.C., *The Old English Finding of the True Cross*, Cambridge (1987).

GRAU, G., *Quellen und Verwandtschaften der älteren germanischen Darstellungen des jüngsten Gerichtes*, Studien zur englischen Philologie, 31, Halle (1908).

MORRIS, R., ed., *Legends of the Holy Rood*, Early English Text Society, Old Series 46, London (1871).

NESTLE, E., *De Sancta Cruce*, Berlin (1889).

RYSSEL, V., 'Syrische Quellen abendländischer Erzählungsstoffe', *Archiv*, xciii (1894), 1–22.

STEVENS, W.O., *The Cross in the Life and Literature of the Anglo-Saxons*, Yale Studies in English 23, New Haven, Connecticut (1904).

STRAUBINGER, J., *Die Kreuzauffindungslegende*, Paderborn (1912).

SWANTON, M., *The Dream of the Rood*, Manchester (1970); revised edition, Exeter (1996).

TIXERONT, L.-J., *Les Origines de l'Église d'Édesse et la Legende d'Abgar*, Paris (1888), pp. 163–75.

CYNEWULF'S ELENE

STUDIES

ANDERSON, E.R., 'Cynewulf's *Elene*: manuscript divisions and structural symmetry', *Modern Philology*, lxxii (1974), 111–22.

——'Cynewulf's *Elene* 1115b–24, the conversion of the Jews: figurative or literal?', *English Language Notes*, xxv (1988), 1–3.

ARNGART, O., 'Some notes on Cynewulf's *Elene*', *English Studies*, xxvii (1946), 19–21

BIGGS, F.M., ' "*Englum gelice*": *Elene* line 1320 and *Genesis A* line 185', *Neuphilologische Mitteilungen*, lxxxvi (1985), 447–52.

BOSSE, R.B. and J.L. WYATT, 'Hrothgar and Nebuchadnezzar: conversion in Old English verse', *Papers on Language and Literature*, xxiii (1987), 257–71.

BREEZE, A., '*Exodus, Elene*, and *The Rune Poem*: *milpæþ* "army road, highway" ', *Notes and Queries*, ccxxxvi (1991), 436–38.

BROWN, C.F., 'Cynewulf and Alcuin', *Publications of the Modern Language Association*, xviii (1903), 308–34.

——'Irish-Latin influence in Cynewulfian texts', *Englische Studien*, xl (1908), 1–29.

BUTLER, S.E., 'The Cynewulf question revived', *Neuphilologische Mitteilungen*, lxxxiii (1982), 15–23.

CALDER, D.G., 'Strife, revelation, and conversion: the thematic structure of *Elene*', *English Studies*, liii (1972), 201–10.

——*Cynewulf*, Boston (1981).

CAMPBELL, J.J., 'Cynewulf's multiple revelations', *Medievalia et Humanistica*, New Series iii (1972), 257–77.

CHERNISS, M.D., 'The oral-traditional opening theme in the poems of Cynewulf', in J.M. FOLEY, et al., ed., *De Gustibus: Essays for Alain Renoir*, New York (1992), pp. 40–65.

COOK, A.S., 'The date of the Old English *Elene*', *Anglia*, xv (1893), 9–20.

COSIJN, P.J., 'Anglosaxonica', *Tijddschrift voor Nederlandsche Taal- en Leiterkunde*, i (1881), 143–48.

——'Cynewulfs Runenverzen', *Verslagen en Mededeelingen der koninklijke Akademie van Wetenschappen*, Series 3, vii (1890), 54–64.

DAS, S.K., *Cynewulf and the Cynewulf Canon*, Calcutta (1942).

DIAMOND, R.E., 'The diction of the signed poems of Cynewulf', *Philological Quarterly*, xxxviii (1959), 228–41.

DILLER, H.-J., 'Pronoun and reference in Old English poetry', in D. KASTOVSKY, ed., *Historical English Syntax*, Berlin (1991), pp. 125–40.

BIBLIOGRAPHY

DOANE, A.N., 'Elene 610a: "Rexgeniðlan"', Philological Quarterly, lviii (1979), 237–40.

DONOGHUE, D., Style in Old English Poetry: the Test of the Auxiliary, New Haven, Connecticut, 1987.

——'Postscript on Style in Old English Poetry', Neuphilologische Mitteilungen, xcii (1991), 405–20.

DOUBLEDAY, J., 'The speech of Stephen and the tone of Elene', in L.E. NICHOLSON, et al., ed., Anglo-Saxon Poetry: Essays in Appreciation for John C. McGalliard, Notre Dame, Indiana (1975), pp. 116–23.

DUBOIS, M.-M., Les Éléments latins dans la Poésie religieuse de Cynewulf, Paris (1943).

ELLIOT, R.W.V., 'Cynewulf's runes in Christ II and Elene', English Studies, xxxiv (1953), 49–57.

EMERSON, O.F., 'The legend of Joseph's bones in Old and Middle English', Modern Language Notes, xiv (1899), 331–34.

ENGBERG, N.J., 'Mod-mægen balance in Elene, The Battle of Maldon and The Wanderer', Neuphilologische Mitteilungen, lxxxv (1984), 212–26.

FAISS, K., 'Gnade' bei Cynewulf und seiner Schule, Tübingen (1967).

FISH, V., 'Theme and pattern in Cynewulf's Elene', Neuphilologische Mitteilungen, lxxvi (1975), 1–25.

FRESE, D.W., 'The art of Cynwulf's runic signatures', in L.E. NICHOLSON, et al., ed., Anglo-Saxon Poetry: Essays in Appreciation for John C. McGalliard, Notre Dame, Indiana (1975), pp. 312–34.

FRY, D.K., 'Themes and type-scenes in Elene 1–113', Speculum, xliv (1969), 35–45.

GARDNER, J., 'Cynewulf's Elene: sources and structure', Neophilologus, liv (1970), 65–76.

GRADON, P.O.E., 'Constantine and the barbarians', Modern Language Review, xlii (1947), 161–72.

——'Cynewulf's Elene and Old English prosody', English and Germanic Studies, ii (1948–49), 10–19.

HARBUS, A., 'Text as revelation: Constantine's dream in Elene', Neophilologus, lxxviii (1994), 645–53.

HARMATIUK, S.J., A Statistical Approach to Some Aspects of Style in Six Old English Poems: A Computer-Assisted Study, Bochum (1980), pp. 89–107.

HERMANN, J.P., 'The theme of spiritual warfare in the Old English Elene', Papers on Language and Literature, xi (1975), 115–25.

HILL, T.D., 'The tropological context of heat and cold imagery in

Anglo-Saxon poetry', *Neuphilologische Mitteilungen*, lxix (1968), 522–32.

——'Sapiential structure and figural narrative in the Old English *Elene*', *Traditio*, xxvii (1971), 159–77.

——'Bread and stone, again: *Elene* 611–18', *Neuphilologische Mitteilungen*, lxxxi (1980), 252–57.

HOLTHAUSEN, F., 'Zu Cynewulfs *Elene*', *Anglia Beiblatt*, xv (1904), 73–74; xvii (1906), 176–78; xviii (1907), 77–78, 204–5.

——'Zur Quelle von Cynwulfs *Elene*', *Zeitschrift für deutsche Philologie*, xxxvii (1905), 1–19.

——'Zur Quelle von Cynwulfs *Elene*', *Archiv*, cxxv (1910), 83–88.

——'Zur Quelle von Cynwulfs *Elene*', *Anglia Beiblatt*, xlv (1934), 93–94.

HOWARD, E.J., '*Elene* [439]', *Modern Language Notes*, xlv (1930), 22.

IRVINE, M., 'Anglo-Saxon literary theory exemplified in Old English poems: interpreting the Cross in *The Dream of the Rood* and *Elene*', *Style*, xx (1986), 157–81; reprinted in K.O. O'KEEFFE, ed., *Old English Shorter Poems: Basic Readings*, New York (1994), pp. 31–63.

KENT, C.W., *Teutonic Antiquities in Andreas and Elene*, Halle (1887).

KERN, J.H., 'Altenglish *eorodciest* und *Elene* 35f.', *Englische Studien*, li (1917), 8–15.

KLAEBER, F., 'Notizen zur Cynewulfs *Elene*', *Anglia*, xxix (1906), 271–72.

——'Cynewulfs *Elene* 1262f.', *Journal of English and Germanic Philology*, vi (1906–7), 197.

KOCK, E.A., 'Jubilee jaunts and jottings: 250 contributions to the interpretation and prosody of Old West Teutonic alliterative poetry', *Lunds Universitets Årsskrift*, New Series 1, xiv (1918), 1–82.

——'Interpretations and emendations of early English texts', *Anglia*, xliii (1919), 298–312; xliv (1920), 245–60; xlvvvii (1923), 264–73.

——'Plain Points and puzzles', *Lunds Universitets Årsskrift*, New Series 1, xvii (1922).

LAMPUGNANI, M., 'Giochi paronomastici nell'*Elena* di Cynewulf: Proposta di analisi tipologica', *Confronto Letterario: Quaderni del Dipartimento di Lingue e Letterature Straniere Moderne dell'Universita di Pavia*, x (1993), 301–17.

LEHMANN, W.P. and V.F. DAILEY, *The Alliterations of the Christ, Guthlac, Elene, Juliana, Fates of the Apostles, Dream of the Rood*, Austin, Texas (1960).

LEIDING, H., *Die Sprache der Cynewulfschen Dichtungen Crist, Juliana und Elene*, Marburg (1888).

BIBLIOGRAPHY

NELSON, M., '*Judith*: A Story of a secular saint', *Germanic Notes*, xxi (1990), 12–13.

——'*Judith, Juliana, and Elene: Three Fighting Saints*, or, How I learned that translators need courage too', *Medieval Perspectives*, ix (1994), 85–98.

OLSEN, A.H., *Speech, Song, and Poetic Craft: The Artistry of the Cynewulf Canon*, New York (1984).

PORTER, N.A., 'Wrestling with loan-words: poetic use of "*engel*", "*seraphim*", and "*cherubim*" in *Andreas* and *Elene*', *Neuphilologische Mitteilungen*, lxxxix (1988), 155–70.

PROLLIUS, M., *Über den syntactischen Gebrauch des Conjunctivs in den Cynewulfschen Dichtungen Elene, Juliana und Crist*, Marburg (1888).

REGAN, C.A., 'Evangelicalism as the informing principle of Cynewulf's *Elene*', *Traditio*, xxix (1973), 27–52.

RICE, R.C., 'The Penitential motif in Cynewulf's *Fates of the Apostles* and in his epilogues', *Anglo-Saxon England*, vi (1977), 105–19.

ROGERS, H.L., 'Rhymes in the epilogue to *Elene*: a reconsideration', *Leeds Studies in English*, v (1971), 47–52.

SCHAAR, C., *Critical Studies in the Cynewulf Group*, Lund Studies in English 17, Lund (1949).

SCHÜRMANN, J., *Darstellung der Syntax in Cynewulfs Elene*, Paderborn (1884).

SHORT, D.D., 'Another look at a point of Old English grammar: *Elene* 508 and Psalm 77:27', *In Geardagum*, v (1983), 39–46.

SISAM, K., 'Cynewulf and his poetry', *Proceedings of the British Academy*, xviii (1932), 303–31; reprinted in *Studies in the History of Old English Literature*, Oxford (1953), pp. 1–28.

SKLUTE, L.M., '*Freoðuwebbe* in Old English poetry', *Neuphilologische Mitteilungen*, lxxi (1970), 534–41.

SMITHSON, G.A., *The Old English Christian Epic: a study in the plot technique of the Juliana, the Elene, the Andreas and the Christ, in comparison with the Beowulf and with the Latin literature of the Middle Ages*, Berkeley, California (1910).

STEPSIS, R. and R. RAND, 'Contrast and conversion in Cynewulf's *Elene*', *Neuphilologische Mitteilungen*, lxx (1969), 273–82.

STRUNK, W., 'Notes on Cynewulf', *Modern Languages Notes*, xvii (1902), 186–87.

SWAEN, A.E.H., 'Notes on Cynewulf's *Elene*', *Anglia*, xvii (1895), 123–24.

TALENTINO, A.V., '"Causing city walls to resound": *Elene* 151b', *Papers on Language and Literature*, ix (1973), 189–93.

TRAUTMANN, M., *Kynewulf der Bischof und Dichter*, Bonn (1899).

——'Zu Cynewulfs Runenstellen', *Bonner Beiträge zur Anglistik*, ii (1899), 118–20.

——'Berichtigungen, Erklärungen und Vermutungen zu Cynewulfs Werken', *Bonner Beiträge zur Anglistik*, xxiii (1907), 85–146.

TUPPER, F., 'The Cynewulfian runes of the religious poems', *Modern Language Notes*, xxvii (1912), 131–37.

TWEEDIE, W.M., 'Kent's *Cynewulf's Elene*', *Modern Language Notes*, vii (1892), 62.

WACK, G., 'Artikel und Demonstrativpronomen in *Andreas* und *Elene*', *Anglia*, xv (1893), 209–20.

WARTH, J. v.d., *Metrisch-Sprachliches und Textkritisches zu Cynewulfs Werken*, Halle (1908).

WATTS, A.C., *The Lyre and the Harp: a comparative reconsideration of oral tradition in Homer and Old English Epic Poetry*, New Haven, Connecticut (1969).

WHATLEY, G., 'Cynewulf and Troy: a note on *Elene* 642–61', *Notes and Queries*, xx (1973), 203–5.

——'Old English onomastics and narrative art: *Elene* 1062', *Modern Philology*, lxxiii (1975), 109–20.

——'Bread and stone: Cynewulf's *Elene* 611–618', *Neuphilologische Mitteilungen*, lxxvi (1975), 550–60.

WHEELER, R., 'A note on æðele spald: *Elene* 297b–300 and John 9 : 1–7', *English Language Notes*, xxv (1987), 7–8.

WINE, J.D., *Figurative Language in Cynewulf: Defining Aspects of a Poetic Style*, New York (1993).

WOLPERS, T., *Die englische Heiligenlegende des Mittelalters. Eine Formegeschichte des Legendenerzählens von der spätantiken lateinischen Tradition bis zur Mitte des 16. Jahrhunderts*, Tübingen (1964).

WOODWORTH, R.B., '*Wendelsæ*', *Modern Language Notes*, vi (1891), 135–36.

WRIGHT, C.D., 'The pledge of the soul: a judgment theme in Old English homiletic literature and Cynewulf's *Elene*', *Neuphilologische Mitteilungen*, xci (1990), 23–30.

WRIGHT, E.F., 'Cynewulf's *Elene* and the "Sinal Sacu"', *Neuphilologische Mitteilungen*, lxxvi (1975), 538–49.

WURFF, W.A.M. van der, 'Cynewulf's *Elene*: The First Speech to the Jews', *Neophilologus*, lxvi (1982), 301–12.

GLOSSARY

In the glossary words will be found under the forms in which they occur in the text, except that nouns and adjectives will be found under the *nom.sg.* and verbs under the infinitive (except that the present forms of 'to be' will be found under *beon*, the pret. forms under *pæs*); pronouns under the nom.sg.m. except the 1st and 2nd pers. of the personal pronouns which will be found under the nom.sg. or nom.pl. Irregular or variant grammatical and phonological forms have cross references to the words under which they are dealt with. References are to lines of the text and are selective only. Italicized references indicate an emendation. An *n* after a line reference indicates a note; a reference preceded by an asterisk a hypothetical form.

The order of the letters is alphabetical; but æ is treated as a separate letter after *a*; þ, ð after *t*. The OE characters ȝ, p are replaced by *g, w*. The prefix *ge-* is ignored in the arrangement of the glossary. Abbreviations are the commonly accepted ones (see *Deor*, ed. Kemp Malone, p. 32, or *Waldere*, ed. F. Norman, p. 49).

Reference is made to the *New English Dictionary* by printing the NED word (under which the OE word is discussed) in square brackets after the headword. No reference is made to the NED when the history of the headword is well-known or when the form in the NED is identical with the headword. Unless otherwise stated the NED reference is to the same part of speech as the headword.

A

ā, *adv.*, always 743, 801, 893.

ābannan, *v.*(7), summon 34.

ābēodan, *v.* (2), offer, announce 87, 1003.

ābrēotan, *v.*(2), [+ BRET]; slay 510.

ac, *conj.*, but 222, 355, 450.

ācennan, *w.v.*(1), [AKEN(NE)²]; give birth to 5; acknowledge 815.

ācīgan, *w.v.*(1), call 603.

geāclian, *w.v.*(2), frighten 57.

ācweðan, *v.*(5), [+ QUETHE]; speak 1071.

ācyrran, *w.v.*(1), [+ CHARE]; turn away 1119.

ād, *m.a-stem*, pyre, fire 585, 950, 1290.

ādrēogan, *v.*(2), [ADREE]; endure 705

āfēdan, *w.v.*(1), rear 913.

āfyrhtan, *w.v.*(1), terrify 56.

āgalan, *v.*(6), [+ GALE¹)]; chant 27.

āgan, *pret-pres.*(7), [OWE], possess 356, 725, 1123, 1181.

āgān, *anom.v.*, depart 1226.

āgangan, *v.*(7), pass 1.

āgen, *adj.*, own 179, 599.

āgifan, *v.*(5), give 167, 455, 587.

āhebban, *v.*(6), raise, rear 10, 17, 353, 837, 861, 867.

āhōn, *v.*(7), [AHANG]; crucify 180, 210, 453, 475n.

āhȳðan, *w.v.*(1), plunder 41.

al, *see* eal(1).

ald, *see* eald.

aldor, *m.a-stem*, [ALDER²]; prince 97.

aldor, *n.a-stem*, life 132; **on aldre**, ever 571; **to aldre**, for ever 349.

85

aldordōm, *m.a-stem*, authority 767

ālesan, *v.*(5), [LEASE¹]; select 286.

ālȳsan, *w.v.*(1), [+ LEESE²]; redeem 181.

āmerian, *w.v.*(1), [+ MERE¹]; purify 1312.

āmetan, *v.*(5), mete out, measure 729, 1247.

ān, *num.adj. pron.*, one 417, 585; ānra gehwylc, each 1287.

anbid, *n.a-stem*, expectation 884n.

ānboren, *p.pt.*, only-begotten 392.

anda, *m.n-stem*, [AND(E)]; vexation 969.

andsæc, *n.a-stem*, [ANDSECH]; opposition, denial 472.

andswaru, *f.ō-stem*, answer 166, 642.

andswerian, *w.v.*(1), answer 396.

andweard, *adj.*, present 630.

andweardlīce, *adv.*, now present 1140.

andwlita, *m.n-stem*, [ANLETH]; face 298.

andwyrde, *n.ja-stem*, [ANDWURDE *v.*]; answer 545.

ānforlǣtan, *v.*(7), relinquish 630, 946.

ānhaga, *m.n-stem*, solitary man 604.

ānhȳdig, *adj.*, resolute 828, 847.

ānmōd, *adj.*, [ANMOD]; unanimous 396.

*āpundrian, *w.v.*(2), adjudge 580n.

ār, *f.ō-stem*, honour 308; mid ārum, ceremoniously 714.

ār, *m.a-stem*, messenger, 76, 737, 995, 1087.

ārǣran, *w.v.*(1), [AREAR]; raise, elate 129, 803.

āreccan, *w.v.*(1), [ARECCHE]; declare 635.

ārfæst, *adj.*, honourable, gracious 12, 512.

ārīsan, *v.*(1), arise 187.

ārlēas, *adj.*, impious 835.

ārwyrðe, *adj.*, venerable 1128.

āsǣlan, *w.v.*(1), [+ SEAL²]; bind 1243.

āscēādan, *v.*(7), [+ SHADE²]; separate from, hold aloof 470, 1313.

āscyrian, *w.v.*(1), separate 1313.

āsēcean, *w.v.*(1), seek out 407, 1018.

āsēoðan, *v.*(2), [+ SEETHE]; purify 1308.

āsettan, *w.v.*(1), set down, accomplish 846, 862, 997.

āspyrigean, *w.v.*(1), [+ SPEER¹]; discover 467.

āstīgan, *v.*(1), [ASTY(E)]; rise 188, 794, 1272.

āsundrian, *w.v.*(2), separate 1309.

ātȳdran, *w.v.*(1), [+ TIDDER¹]; procreate 1279.

āþrēōtan, *v.*(2), irk 368.

āwa, *adv.*, always 950.

āweaxan, *v.*(7), grow 1225.

āweccan, *w.v.*(1), [AWECCHE]; awake, raise up 304, 781, 926.

āweorpan, *v.*(3), [AWARP]; cast out, reject 762, 770.

āwer, *adv.*, anywhere 33.

āwrītan, *v.*(1), write 91.

āwyrgan, *w.v.*(1), [AWARIE]; curse 1299.

Æ

ǣ, *f.i-stem*, law 198.

ǣbylgþ, *f.ō-n.i-stem*, transgression 401 (cp Sievers-Brunner § 255. 3).

ǣclǣca, *m.n-stem*, [EGLECHE a.]; demon, wretch 901.

ǣclēaw, see ǣglēaw.

ǣcræft, *m.a-stem*, knowledge of the law, religion 435.

ǣfen, *n.ja-stem*, evening 139.

86

Æfre, *adv.*, ever 349.

æfst, *mf.i-stem*, [EVEST]; envy 308, 496.

æfter, *prep.w.dat.*, after 233; concerning 675; along, through 135n, 971; for 827.

æghwā, *pron.*, each 1269.

æghwylc, *pron.*, each 1281.

æglǣc, *n.a-stem*, distress 1187.

æglēaw, *adj.*, wise, skilled in law 805; **æclēawe** 321.

æht, *f.i-stem*, [AUGHT¹]; possessions 904, 907, 915.

æht, *f.i-stem*, counsel 473.

ælǣrend, *m.cons-stem*, doctor of the law 506.

ælc, *pron.*, each 1312.

ælfylce, *n.ja-stem*, foreign nation 36.

ælmihtig, *adj.*, almighty 145, 1145.

æne, *adv.*, once 1252.

ænig, *adj.pron.*, any 159, 166, 538, 660, 915.

ænlīc, *adj.*, peerless, beautiful 74, 259.

æpled, *p.pt.*, curved 1259n.

ær, *adv.*, before 74, 101, etc; *superl.* first 116; *conj.*, before 447, 676, etc; *prep.w.dat.*, before 1227; *comp.adj.*, former 305.

ærdæg, *m.a-stem*, dawn 105.

ærgewyrht, *fn.i-stem*, [+ IWURHT]; former deed 1301.

æriht, *n.a-stem*, law 375.

ærþan, *conj.*, until 1083.

æscrōf, *adj.*, illustrious 202, 275.

æscwiga, *m.n-stem*, warrior 259.

æt, *prep.w.dat.*, at 137; from 191; in 1177.

ætsomne, *adv.*, together 833.

ætȳwan, *w.v.(1)*, [ATEW]; reveal, appear 69; **oðȳwde** 163.

æðelcyning, *m.a-stem*, noble king 219.

æðele, *adj.*, [ATHEL]; noble 275, 300, 545, 591, 647, *1028*n, 1073, 1145; *superl.* 476, 732, 1024, 1106, 1173.

æðeling, *m.a-stem*, [ATHELING]; prince, *12*, 66, 99, 202, 845, 885.

æðelu, *n.ja-stem pl.*, [ATHEL]; race, lineage 315, 433.

æwita, *m.n-stem*, lawyer, counsellor 455.

B

bald, *adj.*, bold 412, 593, 1072.

baldor, *m.a-stem*, prince 344.

bān, *n.a-stem*, bone 787.

bāncofa, *m.n-stem*, [+ COVE¹]; body 1249n.

gebann, *n.a-stem*, command 557.

bannan, *v.(7)*, summon 45.

bǣl, *n.a-stem*, pyre 578.

bǣr, *f.ō-stem*, bier 872.

gebǣru, *f.ō-stem*, [IBERE]; behaviour 659, 710.

bæþ, *n.a-stem*, bath 490.

bæðweg, *m.a-stem*, watery path 244.

be, *prep.w.dat.*, concerning 168, 337, 342, etc; by 78; along 1273.

bēacen, *n.a-stem*, sign 92, 100, 162.

beadu, *f.wō-stem*, battle 34.

beadurōf, *adj.*, war-renowned 152, 1003, 1184.

beaduþrēat, *m.a-stem*, [+ THREAT]; army 31.

beaggifa, *m.n-stem*, [BEE² +]; overlord 100, 1198.

bealudǣd, *f.i-stem*, evil deed 515.

bēam, *m.a-stem*, tree, cross 91, 424, 850, 864.

bearhtm, *see* **breahtm.**

bearn, *n.a-stem*, child 179, 181, 354, 476, 525, 813.

bebēodan, *v.(2)*, [BIBEDE]; bid, command, 224, *378*, 710.

bebod, *n.a-stem*, command 1169.

bebūgan, v.(2), [BIBUGH]; avoid 609.

beclingan, v.(3), bind 696.

becuman, v.(4), arrive 142.

bedelfan, v.(3), bury 1080.

bedyrnan, w.v.(1), [+ DERN]; conceal 584, 602.

befæstan, w.v.(1), establish, secure 1212, 1300.

befēolan, v.(3), [BIFELE]; grant 196.

befōn, v.(7), [BEFONG]; grasp 842.

beforan, adv., before 1141; prep. w.dat., before 108.

begangan, v.(7), observe 1170.

bēgen, adj., [BO]; both 614, 618, 804, 963, 1008.

begitan, v.(5), get 1151, 1247n.

begrafan, v.(6), bury 834, 973.

behealdan, v.(7), observe, guard 111, 1143.

behelian, w.v.(1), [BEHELE]; bury, hide 429, 830 (cp Sievers-Brunner § 400 n2).

behlīdan, v.(1), [+ LID sb.]; close 1229.

behȳdan, w.v.(1), conceal 792.

belīōan, v.(1), [+ LITHE¹]; deprive of 877.

belūcan, v.(2), [BELOUKE]; lock up 1026.

bemīōan, v.(1), [+ MITHE]; conceal 583.

bēn, f.i-stem, petition 1088.

benūgan, pret.-pres.(5), have at one's disposal 618.

(ge)bēodan, v.(2), command, offer, announce 18, 80, 276, 971, 1211.

beofian, w.v.(2), [BIVE]; quiver 758.

bēon, anom.v., be 89, 339, 426, 430, 526, 542, 605, 675, 733, 808, 910, 922, 1080, 1295.

beorg, m.a-stem, mountain, sepulchre ? 510, 578.

beorgan, v.(3), [BERGH]; protect 134.

beorhhlīþ, n.a-stem, [+ LITH²]; mountain slope 787.

beorht, adj., fair 88, 489, 782, 789, 821, 1254; comp. 1109; superl. 947; **beorhte,** adv., clearly 92.

beorhtm, see **breahtm.**

beorn, m.a-stem, [BERNE]; man 100, 710.

beran, v.(4), bear, proceed 45n, 1186, 1195n.

berǣdan, w.v.(1), deprive of 498.

berēafian, w.v.(2), deprive of 909.

bescūfan, v.(2), hurl 942.

besēon, v.(5), look 83.

besettan, w.v.(1), surround 1025.

besylcan, w.v.(1), exhaust 697.

betǣcan, w.v.(1), entrust, hand over 585.

betra, see **gōd.**

betwēonum, prep.w.gen., between 1206.

beþeccan, w.v.(1), [BITHECCHE]; cover, overwhelm 76, 835, 1235, 1298.

beþringan, v.(3), [BITHRING]; encompass 949.

beweorcean, w.v.(1), adorn 1023.

beweotigan, w.v.(2), [BIWITIE]; observe 744.

bewindan, v.(3), surround 733.

beþurfan, pret.pres.(3), [+ THARF]; need 543.

bewrecan, v.(5), beat 251n.

(ge)bīdan, v.(1), wait 253, 329, 484, 864, 1092.

biddan, v.(5), pray, ask for 494, 789, 1089.

bigang, mn.a-stem, course 1123.

bill, n.ja-stem, sword 122, 257.

bindan, v.(3), bind 771.

bisceop, m.a-stem, bishop 1051, 1056, 1094.

bisgu, f.ō-stem, affliction 1244.

bisittan, v.(5), possess, hold 473.

bissceophād, *m.ua-stem*, bishopric 1211.

*bitrum, *adv.*, bitterly 1244n.

blāc, *adj.* [BLAKE]; pale, shining 91.

blanca, *m.n-stem*, [BLONK]; steed 1184.

blǣd, *m.a-stem*, [BLEAD]; life, prosperity, joy 354, 489, 825.

blēo, *n.ja-stem*, [BLEE]; form, colour 758, 1105.

blin, *n.a-stem*, cessation 825.

blind, *adj.*, blind 1214.

blindnes, *f.jō-stem*, blindness 299, 389.

blis, *f.jō-stem*, bliss 1137.

geblissian, *w.v.*(*2*), gladden 839.

blīðe, *adj.*, blithe 246, 1317; *comp.* 96.

bōc, *f.monos.-stem*, book 204, 364, 1211.

bōcstæf, *m.a-stem*, letter 91.

boda, *m.n-stem* [BODE¹]; messenger 77, 262.

bodian, *w.v.*(*2*), proclaim 1140.

bold, *n.a-stem*, dwelling, palace 162n.

bord, *n.a-stem*, shield, ship's side, by *synecdoche*, ship? 24n, 114, 238, 1186.

bordhaga, *m.n-stem*, [+ HAW¹]; shield defence 652.

bordhrēða, *m.n-stem*, shield covering ?, phalanx ? 122n.

bōt, *f.ō-stem*, remedy, repentance 299, 1125.

brād, *adj.*, broad 916.

breahtm, *m.a-stem*, tumult, acclaim 39; **bearhtme** 864; **beorhtme** 205n.

gebrec, *n.a-stem*, [+ BRACK¹]; crash 114.

brecan, *v.*(*4*), break, rush 122, 244.

bregdan, *v.*(*3*) [BRAID]; link 257.

brēost, *mn.a-stem*, breast 595.

brēostloca, *m.n-stem*, spirit, heart 1249n.

brēostsefa, *m.n-stem*, mind, spirit 804.

brīdels, *m.a-stem*, bridle 1174.

brīdelshring, *m.a-stem*, bridlering 1193.

brim, *n.a-stem*, sea 253, 971, 1003.

brimþisa, *m.n-stem*, ship 238.

brimwudu, *m.u-stem*, ship 244.

bringan, *v.*(*3*); *w.v.*(*1*), bring 872, 1129, 1137.

brogdenmǣl, *n.a-stem*, [BROWDEN +]; patterned sword 758.

bront, *adj.*, [BRANT]; tall 238.

brōðor, *m.r-stem*, brother 489, 510.

brūcan, *v.*(*2*), enjoy 1250, 1315, 1320.

brytta, *m.n-stem*, [BRIT v.]; giver, ruler 162n, 957.

bryttian, *w.v.*(*2*), [BRIT]; destroy 579.

burg, *f.monos-stem*, city 152, 412, 821, 863.

burgāgend, *m.cons-stem*, prince 1174.

*burgende, *m.ja-stem*, city boundary 31n.

burgsittend, *m.cons-stem*, citizen 276.

burgwīgend, *m.cons-stem*, warrior 34.

būtan, *conj.*, except 661; unless 689; *prep.w.acc.*, except 539; *w.dat.*, without, except for 801, 1227.

byldan, *w.v.*(*1*), [BIELD]; encourage 1038.

bȳme, *f.n-stem*, [BEME]; trumpet 109.

gebyrde, *adj.*, [cp BIRDE]; innate 593.

byrgen, *f.jō-stem* [BURIAN]; tomb 186, 652.

byrne, *f.n-stem*, byrnie 257.

byrnwīggend, *m.cons-stem*, warrior 224; **byrnwīgendum**, 235.

C

cāf, *adj.*, [COF]; swift 56.
campwudu, *m.u-stem*, shield 51.
carcern, *n.a-stem*, prison 715.
cāserdōm, *m.a-stem*, empire 8.
cāsere, *m.ja-stem*, emperor 42, 70, 262.
cearwelm, *m.i-stem*, [+ WALM¹]; surge of grief 1257.
cēas, *f.ō-stem*, conflict 56.
ceaster, *f.ō-stem*, city 274, 384, 972.
ceasterware, *m.i-stem pl.*, citizens 42.
cennan, *w.v.(1)*, give birth to 336, 354, 508; name 587.
cēol, *m.a-stem*, ship 250.
gecēosan, *v.(2)*, choose 607, 1038, 1058.
ceruphīn, cherubim 749.
cild, *n.os.a-stem*, child 336.
cildhād, *m.ua-stem*, childhood 914.
cining, *m.a-stem*, king 988; **cyning** 5, 13, 453, 672.
cirice, *f.n-stem*, church 1007.
cirran, *w.v.(1)*, [CHARE]; turn 914; **cyrrest** 666.
clǣne, *adj.*, pure 96, 749.
geclǣnsian, *w.v.(2)*, [YCLENSE]; cleanse 678, 1034.
cleopigan, *w.v.(2)*, call out, call upon 696, 1099, 1319.
clom, *m.a-stem*, [CLAM¹]; fetter 696.
clynnan, *w.v.(1)*, resound 51.
gecnāwan, *v.(7)*, recognize, perceive 708, 807, 1139.
cnēomǣg, *m.a-stem*, [+ MAY²]; kinsman 587.
cnēow, *n.wa-stem*, knee 847, 1135.
cniht, *m.a-stem*, boy 339.

cnihtgeong, *adj.*, young 640.
cnyssan, *w.v.(1)*, toss 1257.
cōlian, *w.v.(2)*, grow cold 882.
collenferhþ, *adj.*, proud 247.
corðor, *n.a-stem*, company 70, 274.
gecost, *adj.*, [cp CUST¹]; tried, excellent 257, 269, 1185.
cræft, *m.a-stem*, skill, power, knowledge 154, 558, 1017.
cræftig, *adj.*, skilled 314, 315, 419.
crīsten, *adj.*, Christian 979, 988, 1210.
cuman, *v.(4)*, come, 150, 274, 279, 549, 1122, 1303.
cunnan, *pret.-pres.(3)*, know, be able 167, 317, 374, 393, 399, 531, 535, 635, 856, 1162.
cūþ, *adj.*, known 42, 1191.
cwacian, *w.v.(2)*, vibrate 757.
cwalu, *f.ō-stem*, [QUALE¹]; death 499.
***cwānig**, *adj.*, sorrowful 377.
cwealm, *mn.a-stem*, death 676.
gecwēme, *adj.*, [IQUEME]; pleasing 1049.
cwēn, *f.i-stem*, queen, woman 247, 275, 324, 610.
(ge)cweðan, *v.(5)*, [QUETHE]; speak 169, 338, 667, 748, 938.
cwic, *adj.*, alive 691.
cwylman, *w.v.(1)*, [QUELM]; kill 688.
cyme, *m.i-stem*, arrival 41, 1085, 1227.
cyn, *n.ja-stem*, kin 188, 209, 836, 897.
gecynd, *fn.i-stem*, [ICUNDE]; nature 734.
cynestōl, *m.a-stem*, throne 330.
cyning, *see* **cining**.
cyninggenīðla, *m.n-stem*, royal foe 610n.
cyrran, *see* **cirran**.
gecyrran, *w.v.(1)*, [ICHERRE]; change 1060.

(ge)cýðan, w.v.(1), [KITHE]; reveal 161, 409n, 446, 533, 588, 595, 607, 690, 702, 815, 558, 826, 1090.

D

gedafenlic, adj., fitting 1167.

dareðlacende, pres.part., warrior 651; dearedlacende 37.

daroð, m.a-stem, javelin 140n.

dǽd, f.i-stem, deed 386, 1283.

dǽdhwæt, adj., bold 292.

dæg, m.a-stem, day 140, 185, 193n, 312, 358, 485.

dægweorc, n.a-stem, day's work 146

dægweorðung, f.ō-stem, [+ WORTHING[1]]; festival 1233.

dǽl, m.i-stem, part 1298, 1306.

dǽlan, w.v.(1), divide 1286.

dēad, adj., dead 651, 881.

deareðlacende, see dareðlacende.

dēap, m.a-stem, death 187, 477, 584, 606.

dēaðcwalu, f.ō-stem, [+QUALE[1]]; agony 765.

dēgol, n.a-stem, secret 339.

delfan, v.(3), delve 828.

dēma, m.n-stem, judge 745.

dēman, w.v.(1), judge 303, 500.

dēofol, mn.a-stem, devil 181, 900, 1118.

dēofulgild,n.a-stem,idolatry 1040.

dēðgol, see dýgol.

dēop, adj., deep 584, 1189, 1314; dēope, adv., deeply, profoundly 1080.

dēophycggende, 352, dēophycgende, 881, adj., wise.

dēoplice, adv., profoundly, superl. 280.

dēore, see dýre.

dēorlice, adv., worthily, superl. 1158.

dierne, see dyrne.

disig, adj., foolish 477.

dōgor(ge)rim, mn.a-stem, lifetime 705, 779.

dōm, m.a-stem, judgement, Last Judgement, fame 365, 450, 725, 1314.

dōmgeorn, adj., eager for glory 1291.

dōmweorðung, f.ō-stem, honour 146.

(ge)dōn, anom.v., do, put 541, 1158, 1174; send 783.

draca, m.n-stem, dragon 765n.

drēam, m.a-stem, joy 1231.

drenc, m.i-stem, [DRENCH]; drowning 136.

drēogan v.(2), [DREE]; endure 211, 765, 1260.

drifan, v.(1), drive 358.

drūsian, w.v.(2), [DROWSE]; sink, become low 1257.

drȳge, adj., dry 693.

gedryht, f.i-stem, [DRIGHT[1]]; host 27, 736.

dryhten, m.a-stem, [DRIGHTIN]; lord 81, 193, 198, 346, 725.

dryhtlēoþ, n.a-stem, [+ LEOTH]; heroic strain 342.

dryhtscipe, m.i-stem, authority 451.

dūfan, v.(2), pierce 122.

duguþ, f.iō-stem,[DOUTH]; retinue, property 450, 693, 1092; dugoðum 1159.

dūn, f.ō-stem, hill 717.

duru, f.u-stem, door 1229.

gedwola, m.n-stem, [+ DWALE[1]]; error, heresy 371; gedweolan 311n.

dȳgol, adj., [DIGHEL]; secret 541; dēogol 1092.

dynian, w.v.(1), resound 50.

dȳre, adj., precious 292, superl. dēorestan 1233.

dyrnan, w.v.(1), [DERN]; conceal 626, 970.

dyrne, *adj.*, hidden 722, 1092; **dierne** 1080.

dysig, *n.a-stem*, folly 707.

dyslīc, *adj.*, foolish 386.

E

ēac, *adv.*, also 3.

geēacnian, *w.v.(2)*, [cp ECHE]; get with child 341.

ēadhrēðig, *adj.*, blessed 266.

ēadig, *adj.*, [EADI]; blessed 619, 805, 1290.

ēadwela, *m.n-stem*, wealth 1316.

eafera, **eafora**, *m.n-stem*, child 353, 439.

ēage, *n.n-stem*, eye 298.

eald, *adj.*, old 207, 455, 904; **ald** 252, 1265; *comp.* 159; *yldra*, father 462; *yldra fæder*, ancestor, grandfather 436.

ealdfēond, *m.cons-stem*, ancient foe 493.

ealdgewin, *n.a-stem*, ancient conflict 647.

eal(l), *adj.*, all 26, 187, 385, 422, 483, 486, 649, 728, 730, 752, 855, 1087, 1117, 1130, 1196, 1219; **al(l)ra** 645, 815; **eallre** 446; **eallra** 370; *adv.*, wholly 1311.

earc, *f.ō-stem*, ark 399.

eard, *m.au-stem*, [ERD]; dwelling 599.

eare, *see* **geare**.

earfeþe, *n.ja-stem*, [ARVETH *a.*]; distress, torture 700.

earhfaru, *f.ō-stem*, arrow flight, attack 44, 116.

earhgeblond, *n.a-stem*, sea 239.

earm, *m.a-stem*, arm 1235.

earn, *m.a-stem*, [ERNE]; eagle 29.

geearnian, *w.v.(2)*, deserve 526.

ēastweg, *m.a-stem*, road to the east 255.

eatol, *adj.*, [ATEL]; terrible 901.

ēaðe, *adv.*, [EATH]; easily 1292.

ēaðmēdu, *f.ō-stem*, [EDMEDE]; humility 1087.

eaxlgestealla, *m.n-stem*, companion 64.

ebrisc, *adj.*, Hebrew 724; **ebreisce** 397; **ebresce** 559.

ēce, *adj.*, [ECHE]; eternal 526, 745, 799, 801; *adv.*, eternally 1217.

ednīowunga, *adv.*, afresh 300.

ēdre, *adv.*, forthwith 649.

(ge)efnan, *w.v.(1)*, perform 713, 1014.

eft, *adv.*, again, afterwards 143, 1154.

egesa, *m.n-stem*, [cp EISFUL *a.*]; terror 82; **eg(e)san** 57n, 321, 1128.

ēgstrēam, *m.a-stem*, river, sea 66, 241.

ēhtan, *w.v.(1)*, pursue, persecute 139, 927.

elde, *see* **ilde**.

ēleð, *m.a-stem*, fire *1294n*.

ellen, *mn.-a-stem*, strength, courage 724n.

elþēod, *f.ō-stem*, [+ THEDE]; foreign nation 139.

elþēodig, *adj.*, foreign 57, 907.

ende, *m.ja-stem*, end, edge 59, 590.

endelīf, *n.a-stem*, death 585.

enge, *adj.*, narrow, cruel 712, 920, 1261n.

engel, *m.a-stem*, angel 79, 622.

engelcyn, *n.ja-stem*, order of angels 732.

eoforcumbul, *n.a-stem*, [EVER +]; boar image, helmet, 259; **eofurcumble** 76.

eofot, *n.a-stem*, sin 423.

eofulsæc, *n.a-stem*, blasphemy 524.

eorcnanstān, *m.a-stem*, jewel 1024.

ēoredcest, *f.i-stem*, army, legion 36.

eorl, *m.a-stem*, warrior, man 12, 66, 225, 256.

eorlmægen, *n.a-stem*, host of men 980.

eorne, *see* georne.

eorre, *see* yrre.

eorðcyning, *m.a-stem*, earthly king 1173.

eorðe, *f.n-stem*, earth 591, 727, 752.

eorðweg, *m.a-stem*, earthly way 735, 1014.

ēower, *adj.*, your 305, 315, 375, 579.

ermðu, *see* yrmðu.

ēst, *f.i-stem*, [ESTE]; grace 985.

ēðe, *adj.*, [EATH]; pleasant, *superl.* 1294.

ēðel, *m.a-stem*, native land 1219.

ēðgesȳne, *adj.*, clearly visible 256.

eðigean, *w.v.(2)*, [ETHE¹]; exhale, rise up 1106n.

F

fācensēaru, *n.wa-stem* [FAKEN]; treachery 721n.

fāh, *adj.*, [FOE]; guilty 768.

fāmig, *adj.*, foamy 237.

(ge)faran, *v.(6)*, go, die 21, 27, 733, 871, 1273.

fæc, *n.a-stem*, [FEC]; space of time 272, 959.

fǣcne, *adj.*, deceitful, old ? 577, 1236n.

fæder, *m.r-stem*, father 343, 388, 398, 438n, 783, 890.

fæderlīc, *adj.*, paternal 431.

fǣge, *adj.*, doomed 117.

fæger, *adj.*, fair 98, 742, 890, 910, 948; *comp.* 242.

fægere, *adv.*, fairly, well 1212.

fǣle, *adj.*, [FELE²]; true 88.

(ge)fær, *n.a-stem*, expedition 68, 93.

fæst, *adj.*, firm, fast 252, 722, 770, 882, 908; *adv.*, fæste, fast, firmly 570.

fæsten, *n.ja-stem*, strong-hold, place of safety 134n.

fæstlīce, *adv.*, firmly 427; *comp.* 796.

gefæstnian, *w.v.(2)*, fasten 1067.

fæt, *n.a-stem*, vessel 1025.

fæðm, *m.a-stem*, bosom, embrace 728, 765n.

fæðmian, *w.v.(2)*, encircle 971.

fēa, *adj.*, few 174, 817.

gefēa, *m.n-stem*, joy 195, 869.

feala, *adv.*, [FELE]; many 362, 636.

feallan, *v.(7)*, fall 127, 651.

fearoðhengest, *m.a-stem*, ship 226.

feng, *m.i-stem*, embrace 1287.

fēogan, *w.v.(3)*, hate 356, 360.

feohgestrēon, *n.a-stem*, [FEE¹ + ISTREON]; treasure 910.

gefeoht, *n.a-stem*, [IFIHT]; battle 646, 1183.

gefēon, *v.(5)*, rejoice 110, 174, 1115.

fēond, *m.cons-stem*, enemy 68, 93, 207.

fēondscipe, *m.i-stem*, enmity 356.

feor, *adv.*, distant 830; long ago; *comp.* 646.

feorh, *mn.ua-stem*, life, spirit 134, 680; on wīdan fēore, ever 1288; tō wīdan fēore, for ever 211.

feorhlegu, *f.ō-stem*, death 458.

feorhneru, *f.ō-stem*, salvation 897.

feorran, *adv.*, [FERREN]; from afar 992.

fēower, *num.adj.*, four 743.

(ge)fēran, *w.v.(1)*, [FERE-]; go, travel 215, 735.

ferhþ, *see* fyrhþ.

ferhðglēaw, *adj.*, wise 327, 880.

ferhðsefa, *see* firhðsefa.

(ge)ferian, *w.v.(1)*, [FERRY]; carry 108, 992.

gefeti(ge)an, *w.v.(2)*, fetch 1052, 1160.

fēða, *m.n-stem*, battle-formation 35n.

fēðegest, *m.i-stem*, stranger 844.

gefic, *n.a-stem*, deceit 577.

fifelwāeg, *m.i-stem*, sea 237.

fīfhund, *num.*, five hundred 379.

findan, *v.(3)*, find 84, 202, 327, 373, 632, 830, 924, 973, 1031, 1079, 1254.

finger, *m.a-stem*, finger 120.

fīras, *m.ja-stem pl.*, men 897.

firen, *f.ō-stem*, sin 908, 1314.

firhōsefa, *m.n-stem*, mind 213; **fyrhōsefan** 98, 534; **ferhōsefan** 316.

fiðre, *n.ja-stem*, wing 742.

flān, *m.a-f.ō-stem*, [FLANE]; arrow 117.

flēogan, *v.(2)*, fly 140.

flēon, *v.(2)*, flee 127.

fliht, *m.i-stem*, flight 743.

geflit, *n.a-stem*, strife 443.

flōd, *mn.ua-stem*, water 1269.

flot, *n.a-stem*, [FLOAT]; sea 226.

fodder, *n.a-stem*, fodder 360.

folc, *n.a-stem*, folk 27, 117, 157, 362, 415, 1142.

folcscearu, *f.ō-stem*, nation 967; **folcscere** 402.

foldbūend, *m.cons-stem*, dweller on earth 1013.

folde, *f.n-stem*, [FOLD¹]; earth 721.

foldgrǣf, *n.a-stem*, grave 844.

foldweg, *m.a-stem*, road 215.

folgaþ, *m.a-stem*, retinue 903.

folgian, *w.v.(2)*, follow 929.

folm, *f.ō-stem*, hand 1065, 1075.

for, *prep.w.acc.*, before 546; *w.dat.*, in front of 110; on account of 496; **for worulde**, in the world 4; **for eorðan**, on earth 591.

foran, *adv.*, [FORNE]; in front *1183*.

fore, *prep.w.dat.*, before 577; **fore**, *adv.*, before 345n.

foreþanc, *m.a-stem*, deliberation 356.

forgifan, *v.(5)*, give 144, 354.

forlǣran, *w.v.(1)*, seduce 208.

forlǣtan, *v.(7)*, leave, allow 432n, 598, 689, 700, 712, 792, 928.

forniman, *v.(4)*, [FORNIM]; destroy, consume 131, 578n.

forsēcan, *w.v.(1)*, afflict 932.

forsēon, *v.(5)*, despise 389, 1318.

fortyhtan, *w.v.(1)*, [FORTIHT]; lead astray 208.

forþ, *adv.*, forth, thenceforth 120, 192.

forþan, *adv.*, therefore 309.

forþryccan, *w.v.(1)*, [+THRUTCH]; oppress 1276.

forōsnotter, *adj.*, very wise 379; **forōsnoterne** 1052.

forþylman, *w.v.(1)*, envelop 766.

forwyrd, *f.i-stem*, perdition 764.

fōt, *m.monos-stem*, foot 1065.

fōtmǣl, *n.a-stem*, foot 830.

fram, *prep.w.dat.*, from 140; **from** 590; by means of 190.

frǣtwan, *w.v.(1)*, adorn 1198.

frǣtwe, *f.ō-stem pl.*, adornment 88, 1270.

gefrǣtwian, *w.v.(2)*, adorn 742.

frēa, *m.n-stem*, lord 488, 680, 1307.

frēcne, *adj.*, terrible 93.

(ge)fremman, *w.v.(1)*, [FREME]; do, achieve, express an emotion 299, 363, 386, 402, 415, 472, 515, 524, 569.

gefrēge, *adj.*, renowned 967.

frēobearn, *n.a-stem*, child of noble birth 672.

frēond, *m.cons-stem*, friend 360, 953.

frēondlēas, *adj.*, friendless 924.

frēondrǣdden, *f.jō-stem*, friendship 1207.

94

freoðian, *w.v.*(2), [FRITH¹]; protect 1146.

fricca, *m.n-stem*, herald 54.

(ge)fricg(g)an, *v.*(5), ask, learn 155, 157, 560, 990.

frīge, *f.ō-stem pl.*, love 341.

(ge)frignan, *v.*(3), [FRAYNE]; ask, learn 172, 443, 534, 542, 589, 1013.

friþ, *m.u-n.a-stem*, protection 1183.

friðeleās, *adj.*, savage 127.

friðowebba, *m.n-stem*, angel 88.

frōd, *adj.*, wise 343, 431, 443, 542, 637, 1163.

frōfor, *f.ō-stem*, [FROVER]; comfort 196, 502, 1036.

from, *adj.*, bold 261.

from, *prep.*, see fram.

fromlīce, *adv.*, boldly 454.

fruma, *m.n-stem*, [FRUME]; beginning 1141; prince 210; author 771, 792, 838.

frymþ, *f.ō-stem*, [FRUMTH]; beginning, creation 502; frumþa 345.

ful, *adj.*, full 751, 938; *adv.*, fully 167.

fūl, *n.a-stem*, foulness, guilt 768n.

gefullæstan, *w.v.*(1), [FILST]; help 1150.

fultum, *m.a-stem*, help 1052.

gefulwian, *w.v.*(2), [FULL¹]; baptize 1043.

fulwiht, *mn.a-f.i-stem*, [FULLOUGHT]; baptism 172, 490.

furðum, *adv.*, [FORTHEN]; just; syððan furþum, as soon as 913.

furður, *adv.*, further, more 388.

fūs, *adj.*, [FOUS]; ready 1218, 1236.

(ge)fylgan, *w.v.*(1), follow, persist in 371, 576.

fyllan, *w.v.*(1), lay low 1040.

gefyllan, *w.v.*(1), fill, fulfil 680, 1070, 1083, 1142.

fȳr, *n.a-stem*, fire 1105, 1311.

fȳrbæþ, *n.a-stem*, fire-bath 948.

fyrd, *f.i-stem*, [FERD¹]; army 35.

fyrdhwæt, *adj.*, brave 21.

fyrdlēoþ, *n.a-stem*, battle song 27.

fyrdrinc, *m.a-stem*, [+ RINK¹]; warrior 261.

fȳrhāt, *adj.*, fire-hot 936.

fyrhþ, *mn.a-stem*, mind, spirit 196; ferhð 174, 427; wīdan fyrhð, for ever 760; wīdan ferhð 800.

fyrhðsefa, see firhðsefa.

fyrhðwērig, *adj.*, sad, wretched 560.

fyrmest, *adv.*, first, especially 68, 316.

fyrn, *adv.*, [FERN]; long since 632.

fyrndagas, *m.a-stem pl.*, former days 398.

fyrngeflit, *n.a-stem*, ancient strife 903.

fyrngemynd, *f.i-n.ja-stem*, memory of former times 327.

fyrngewrit, *n.a-stem*, ancient record 155, 431.

fyrngid, *n.ja-stem*, ancient lore 542.

fyrnwita, *m.n-stem*, prophet, sage 1153; fyrnweota 343; fyrnwiota 438.

fyrst, *m.ia-stem*, [FRIST]; period of time 67, 490.

fyrstmearc, *f.ō-stem*, appointed interval 1033.

fyrwet, *n.ja-stem*, anxiety 1078.

(ge)fȳsan, *w.v.*(1), [FUSE¹]; hasten, make eager, drive on 226, 260, 1269.

G

gād, *n.wa-stem*, lack 991.

galan, *v.*(6), chant, cry 52, 124n.

galdor, *n.a-stem*, [GALDER]; speech 161.

galga, *m.n-stem*, gallows, cross 179.

gamel, *adj.*, old 1246.

gān, *anom.v.*, go 320, 1095.

gang, *m.a-stem*, course 633, 1255; **gongum**, 648.

gangan, *v.(7)*, go 313.

gār, *m.a-stem*, [GARE¹]; spear 23, 118.

gārþracu, *f.ō-stem*, battle 1185.

gārþrīst, *adj.*, [+ THRISTE]; bold 204.

gāst, *m.a-stem*, spirit 176, 182, 199, 302, 352, 471, 935.

gāstgerȳne, *n.ja-stem*, spiritual mystery 189.

gāsthālig, *adj.*, holy in spirit 562.

gāstlēas, *adj.*, dead 874.

gāstsunu, *m.u-stem*, spiritual son 673.

gǣlan, *w.v.(1)*, [GELE]; hesitate 692.

ge…ge, *conj.*, both…and 964–5.

gē, *pron.*, ye 290, 293, 295, 298, 309, *318*.

geador, *adv.*, together 26.

geagncwide, *see* **gēncwide**.

geagninga, *adv.*, completely 673.

gēar, *n.a-stem*, year 1, 7, 1264.

geāra, *adv.*, [YORE]; formerly 1265.

geārdagas, *m.a.stem pl.*, former days 290, 1266.

geare, 167, **eare**, 399, **gere**, 859, **gearwe**, 1239, *adv.*, [YARE]; clearly, completely, exactly; *comp.* 945; *superl.* 328.

gearolīce, *adv.*, completely 288.

gearu, *adj.*, [YARE]; ready 23, 85 222, 605.

gearusnottor, *adj.*, very wise 586; **gearosnotor** 418.

gearwe, *see* **geare**.

(ge)gearwian, *w.v.(2)*, [YARE]; prepare, provide 47, 888, 999.

gēāsne, *adj.*, [GEASON]; lacking 923.

geatolīc, *adj.*, magnificent 258, 331.

gehðu, *f.ō-stem*, [cp GETHE]; sorrow, anxiety 609, 667; **gehdum** 531n.

gēn, *adv.*, again, still 373, 1077.

gēncwide, *m.i-stem*, [+ QUIDE]; answer 594; **geagncwide** 525.

gēoc, *f.ō-stem*, help 1138.

gēocend, *m.cons-stem*, helper 682.

geofen, *n.a-stem*, ocean 227.

geogoþ, *f.ō-stem*, youth 638, 1264.

geogoðhād, *m.ua-stem*, youth 1266.

geolorand, *m.a-stem*, shield *yellow because made of linden wood or decorated with gold* 118.

gēomor, *adj.*, [YOMER]; sorrowful 182, 322, 627, 921.

gēomormōd, *adj.*, sorrowful 413.

geond, *prep.w.acc.*, [YOND]; throughout 16; through 733.

georn, *adj.*, [YERN]; eager 268.

georne, 199, 1162, **eorne** 322, *adv.*, eagerly, well.

geornlīce, *adv.*, eagerly 1096.

gēotan, *v.(2)*, [YET, YOTE]; pour out 1132.

gere, *see* **geare**.

gidd, *n.ja-stem*, [YED]; song, traditional knowledge 418, 586.

gif, *conj.*, if 435, 441, 459.

gifan, *v.(5)*, give 360n, 365.

gifu, *f.ō-stem*, gift, grace 176, 265, 1143.

gildan, *v.(3)*, repay 493.

gim, *m.a-stem*, gem 90.

gīman, *w.v.(1)*, [YEME]; heed 616.

gimcynn, *n.ja-stem*, precious stone 1023.

gīna, *adv.*, again; þa **gīna**, yet again 1069.

ging, *adj.*, young 353, 464; *comp.* 159.

gīō, *adv.*, formerly 436.

girwan, *w.v.(1)*, build 1021.

gīsel, *m.a-stem*, [YISEL]; hostage 600.

glǣd, *adj.*, glad; *comp.* 955.

glǣdmŏd, *adj.*, joyful 1095.

glǣm, *m.i-stem*, radiance 1266.

gleǣw, *adj.*, [GLEW]; wise 594, 638, 806, 1162; *superl.* 536.

gleǣwhȳdig, *adj.*, wise 934.

gleǣwlīce, *adv.*, wisely 189.

gleǣwnes, *f.jō-stem*, wisdom 961.

glēd, *f.i-stem*, [GLEED]; fire-coal 1302.

geglengan, *w.v.(1)*, adorn 90.

gnornian, *w.v.(2)*, grieve 1259.

gnornsorg, *f.ō-stem*, grief 655, 976.

gnyrn, *f.i-stem*, grief, sin *422*, 1138.

gnyrnwrǣc, *f.jō-stem*, [+ WRECHE]; vengeance for grief 359.

god, *m.a-stem*, God 4, 109, 209, 961.

gŏd, *adj.*, good 637; *comp.* betera 506, 618, 1038; *superl.* sēlest, sēlost, sēlust, 527, 1018, 1027, 1164, *1169*, 1201.

gŏd, *n.a-stem*, goods, property 923.

godbearn, *n.a-stem*, divine son 719.

godcund, *adj.*, divine 1032.

gŏddend, *m.cons-stem*, benefactor 359.

godgim, *m.a-stem*, divine jewel, sun, heavenly body 1113n.

godspel, *n.a-stem*, gospel 176.

gold, *n.a-stem*, gold 90, 1259, 1309.

goldhoma, *m.n-stem*, [+HAME¹]; garment ornamented with gold 991.

goldhord, *m.a-stem*, treasure 790.

goldwine, *m.i-stem*, overlord 201.

gomen, *n.a-stem*, joy 1264.

gong, *see* gang.

gram, *adj.*, [GRAME]; fierce 43, 118.

grǣp, *f.ō-stem*, [GROPE¹]; grip 759.

grēŏt, *n.a-stem*, earth 834.

grim, *adj.*, grim 525.

grīma, *m.n-stem*, helmet 125.

grīmhelm, *m.a-stem*, visored helmet 258.

gring, *mn.a-stem*, slaughter 115.

gringan, *v.(3)*, fall 126.

gripe, *m.i-stem*, grip 1302.

grund, *m.ua-stem*, ground, abyss, world 943, 1113, 1289.

gryrefæst, *adj.*, [GRURE +]; terrible 759.

guma, *m.n-stem*, [GOME¹]; man 14, 464, 531, 562.

gumrīce, *n.ja-stem*, [+ RICHE]; earthly kingdom 1220.

gūþ, *f.ō-stem*, battle 23.

gūðcwēn, *f.i-stem*, warlike queen 254.

gūðgelǣca, *m.n-stem*, warrior 43.

gūðheard, *adj.*, brave in battle 204.

gūðrŏf, *adj.*, courageous 273.

gūðscrūd, *n.monos-stem*, coat-of-mail 258.

gūðwearð, *m.a-stem*, prince 14.

gylden, *adj.*, golden 125.

gylt, *m.i-stem*, guilt 816.

H

habban, *w.v.(3)*, have 49, 63, 288, 316, 369, 408, 415, 594, 621, 807, 824, 1252.

hǣd, *m.ua-stem*, form, manner, order of being 72, 336, 739n, 1245n.

hǣdor, *n.a-stem*, brightness 629n.

half, *see* healf.

hǣlig, *adj.*, holy 86, 107, 218, 333, 364, 429, 457, 625, 720, 739, 750, 757, 820, 842, 975, 987, 1005, 1011, 1031, 1093, 1194.

hǣm, *m.a-stem*, home 143, 920.

hand, *f.u-stem*, hand 457, 804.

handgeswing, n.a-stem, combat 115.

hāt, n.a-stem, heat 628.

hāt, adj., hot 1132, 1297; superl. 579.

hātan, v.(7), [HIGHT¹]; command, call, name 42, 214, 505, 755, 1172.

hǣdor, adj., clear 747.

hæft, m.a-stem, captivity 703.

gehæftan, w.v.(1), [cp HAFT²]; oppress 613.

hæftnēd, f.i-stem, imprisonment 297.

hǣl, n.i-stem, [HEAL]; greeting 1002.

hǣlend, m.cons-stem, [HEALEND]; saviour 725, 808, 1062.

hæleþ, m.cons-stem, [HELETH]; warrior, man 73, 273, 511, 538, 640, 661, 671.

hǣlo, f.ō-stem, health 1215.

hǣs, f.i-stem, [HEST]; command 86.

hǣðen, adj., heathen 126, 1075.

hē, hēo, hit, pron., he, she, it 9, 14, 18, 147, 170, 271, 350, 440 (reflexive), 677 895; hēo 570; hīo 268; hire 1199; hiere 222; pl. 48, 173, 360, 998; he 59n; hīo 384; hēo 254; hiera 360; hira 174.

hēafodwylm, m.i-stem, tears 1132.

hēah, adj., high 424; superl. 197n.

hēahengel, m.a-stem, archangel 750.

hēahmægen, n.a-stem, sublime power 464, 752.

(ge)healdan, v.(7), hold, observe guard 156, 192, 449, 823, 1168.

healf, f.ō-stem, side 548, 1179; halfa 954.

healfcwic, adj., half dead 133.

healsian, w.v.(2), [HALSE¹]; beseech 699.

healt, adj., halt 1214.

hēan, adj., [HEAN]; wretched 701, 1215.

hēannes, f.jō-stem, height 1124.

hēap, m.a-stem, band, throng, 141, 269, 1205.

heard, adj., cruel 83, 115, 180, 557, 704, 808; comp. 565; hearde, adv., severely 400.

heardecg, f.jō-stem, sword 757.

hearding, m.a-stem, warrior 25.

hearm, m.a-stem, grief 911.

hearmloca, m.n-stem, prison 695.

heaðofremmende, pres.part., fighting 130.

geheaðrian, w.v.(2), confine 1275.

heaðuwylm, m.i-stem, fierce flame 1305; heaðowelma 579.

hebban, v.(6), raise 25, 107, 123.

hel, f.jō-stem, hell 900.

helan, v.(4), [HELE¹]; conceal 703.

helm, m.a-stem, covering, defender 148, 230n.

help, f.ō-stem, help 679, 1031.

hēo, n.ja-stem, form 6.

heofon, m.a-stem, heaven 699, 727, 1229; heofun 752; heofenum 83.

heofoncining, m.a-stem, 747; king of heaven; heofoncyninges 170; heofoncyninge 367.

heofonlīc, adj., heavenly 739, 1144.

heofonrīce, n.ja-stem, [HEAVEN-RIC]; heavenly kingdom 197, 621.

heofonsteorra, m.n-stem, heavenly body 1112.

heolster, mn.a-stem, [HOLSTER]; darkness, concealment 1081.

heolstorhof, m.a-stem, hell 763n.

heorte, f.n-stem, heart 628, 1223.

heorucumbul, n.a-stem, standard 107.

heorudrēorig, adj., wounded or very sorrowful 1214.

heorugrim, *adj.*, very fierce *119*.

hĕr, *adv.*, here 661.

here, *m.ja-stem*, [HERE]; army 32, 52, 58, 65, 101, 115, 143, 148, 205, 406.

herecombol, *n.a-stem*, battle standard 25.

herefeld, *m.ua-stem*, battlefield *126*, 269.

heremægen, *n.a-stem*, multitude 170.

hereme&ögel, *n.a-stem*, assembly 550.

hererǽswa, *m.n-stem*, leader 994.

heresīþ, *m.a-stem*, campaign 133.

heretēma, *m.n-stem*, leader 10.

hereprēat, *m.a-stem*, army 265.

hereweorc, *n.a-stem*, warfare 656.

herian, *w.v.(1)*, [HERY]; praise 453, 892, 1096, 1220; herigean 919.

herwan, *see* (ge)hyrwan.

hete, *m.i-stem*, [HATE¹]; hatred 424.

hetend, *m.cons-stem*, enemy 18, 119.

hīehðo, *f.ō-stem*, height 1086.

gehigd, *fn.i-stem*, thought 1223.

hige, 808, 840, hyge, 685, *m.i-stem*, [HIGH¹]; mind, thought.

higefrōfor, *f.ō-stem*, consolation 355.

higegeōmor, 1297, hygegēomre 1215, *adj.*, sad.

higeglēaw, *adj.*, wise 333.

higeþanc, *m.a-stem*, thought 156.

hild, *f.jō-stem*, battle 18, 32.

hildedēōr, *adj.*, bold in battle 935.

hildegesa, *m.n-stem*, terror in battle 113.

hildenǽdre, *f.n-stem*, battle serpent, arrow 119, 141.

hilderinc, *m.a-stem*, warrior 263.

hildeserce, *f.n-stem*, coat-of-mail 234.

hildfruma, *m.n-stem*, prince, leader 10.

hīwbeorht, *adj.*, radiant 73.

gehladan, *v.(6)*, [LADE]; load 234.

hlāf, *m.a-stem*, loaf 613, 616.

hlāford, *m.a-stem*, lord 265, 475.

hlǽfdige, *f.n-stem*, lady 400.

hleahtor, *m.a-stem*, exultation 919.

hlēapan, *v.(7)*, run 54.

hlēo, *mn.wa-stem*, [LEE¹]; refuge, protection 99, 507, 616, 1073.

hlēor, *n.a-stem*, [LEER¹]; face 1098.

hlēōðrian, *w.v.(2)*, cry out 900.

gehlēða, *m.n-stem*, companion 113.

hlihan, *v.(6)*, rejoice 994.

hlūd, *adj.*, loud 1272; hlūde, *adv.*, loudly, clearly 406.

hlȳt, *m.i-stem*, portion 820.

hnāg, *adj.*, humiliating 668.

hnesce, *adj.*, [NESH]; soft 615.

hof, *n.a-stem*, [HOVE³]; house 557.

holm, *m.a-stem*, sea 982.

holmþracu, *f.ō-stem*, stormy sea 727.

holt, *mn.a-stem*, forest 113.

hōn, *v.(7)*, hang 424, 851.

hord, *n.a-stem*, treasure 1091.

horh, *mn.a-stem*, [HORE]; filth; *instr.* 297.

hornbora, *m.n-stem*, trumpeter 54.

hospcwide, *m.i-stem*, [+QUIDE]; insult, blasphemy 523.

hrā, *mn.wa-stem*, body, corpse 579.

hrædlīce, *adv.*, [RADLY]; quickly 1086.

hraðe, 76, raðe, 372, *adv.*, [RATHE]; quickly.

hrefen, 52, hrefn, 110, *m.a-stem*, raven.

hrēmig, *adj.*, exultant 149, 1137.

hrēof, *adj.*, [REOF]; leprous 1214.

hrēosan, *v.(2)*, [REOSE]; fall 763.

hreðer, *m.a-stem*, breast 1144.

hreðerloca, *m.a-stem*, breast 86n.

99

hring, *m.a-stem*, globe 1131n.
hringedstefna, *m.n-stem*,
 [+ STEM]; ring-prowed ship
 248.
hrōf, *m.a-stem*, roof 89.
hrōpan, *v.*(7), [ROPE²]; call out,
 make a proclamation 54.
hrōr, *adj.*, [cp ROAR sb.²]; bold
 65.
hrōðer, *m.a-stem*, comfort 16.
hrūse, *f.n-stem*, earth 218.
hū, *conj.adv.*, how 176, 179, 185,
 335.
hund, *num.*, hundred 2.
hungor, *m.ua-stem*, hunger 613,
 616.
hūru, *conj.*, [HURE]; indeed 1046.
hūs, *n.a-stem*, house 880, 1236n.
hūþ, *f.ō-stem*, plunder 149.
hwā, hwæt, *pron.*, who, what
 161n, 400; *w.gen.*, what kind of
 902; to hwan, to what purpose
 1157.
gehwā, *pron.*, each 358, 569, 972,
 1228.
hwǣr, *conj.*, where 205, 217, 429,
 563.
gehwǣr, *adv.*, everywhere 1182.
hwæt, *adj.*, [WHAT²]; active 22.
hwæt, *interj.*, [WHAT¹]; lo 293,
 334, 364, etc.
hwætēadig, *adj.*, fortunate 1194.
hwætmōd, *adj.*, bold 1005.
gehwæðer, *pron.*, each of two
 628, 963.
hwæðre, *adv.*, however 719.
gehweorfan, *v.*(3), [WHARVE];
 turn 1125.
hwīl, *f.ō-stem*, space of time 479;
 hwīle nū, just now 582.
hwīt, *adj.*, white 73.
hwone, *conj.*, until 254.
hwōpan, *v.*(7), threaten 82n.
hwylc, *pron.*, which 850, 857.
gehwylc, *pron.*, each, every 278,
 319, 409, 598, 1283, 1310, 1313.

hwyrft, *m.i-stem*, course 1.
(ge)hȳdan, *w.v.*(1), [IHEDE]; hide
 218, 831, 1091, 1107.
hyder, *adv.*, hither 548.
hyge, *see* hige.
hygegēomor, *see* higegēomor.
hygerūn, *f.ō-stem*, secret of the
 heart 1098.
hyht, *m.i-stem*, [HIGHT²]; hope
 197n, 797.
hyhtful, *adj.*, hopeful 922.
hyhtgifa, *m.n-stem*, giver of hope
 851.
gehȳnan, *w.v.*(1), [HEAN]; humble
 720.
hȳnðu, *f.ō-stem* humiliation 210.
(ge)hȳran, *w.v.*(1), hear, obey
 333, 364, 442, 511, 538, 572, 709,
 784, 838, 1001, 1209.
hyrde, *m.ja-stem*, shepherd 348.
hyrst, *f.i-stem*, ornament 263.
gehyrstan, *w.v.*(1), adorn 331.
(ge)hyrwan, *w.v.*(1), despise 221,
 355, 387.
hyse, *m.i-stem*, boy 523.
hȳþ, *f.jō-stem*, [HITHE]; harbour
 248.
gehȳwan, *see* geȳwan.

I

ic, *pron.*, I, 163, 164, 240, 288, 347,
 361, 469.
īcan, *w.v.*(1), [ECHE]; increase
 904.
ides, *f.iō-stem* lady 229, 241, 405.
geīewan, *see* geȳwan.
ilca, *adj.*, same 183, 436.
ilde, *m.i-stem pl.*, men 521; elda
 476; yldum 791.
in, *prep. w.acc.*, into 6; in 336;
 w.dat., in 177, on 330; into 1296.
in, *adv.*, in 122.
inbryrdan, *see* onbryrdan.
ingemynd, *f.i-n.ja-stem*, remembrance 1252.

100

ingemynde, *adj.*, present to the mind 895.

ingeþanc, *m.a-stem*, purpose 680.

innan, *adv.*, within 1056.

innoð, *m.a-stem*, [INNETH]; heart 1145.

instæpes, *adv.*, forthwith 127.

inwit, *n.a-stem*, guile 207.

inwitþanc, *m.a-stem*, malice 308.

inwrēon, *see* onwrēon.

L

lă, *interj.*, lo 902.

lăc, *n.a-f.o-stem*, [LAKE¹]; gift 1136, 1199.

lăcan, *v.*(7), [LAKE¹]; fly, leap up 580, 899.

lagofæsten, 249, lagufæsten, 1016, *n.ja-stem*, water fastness.

lagostrēam, *m.a-stem*, river 137.

lama, *m.n-stem*, lame man 1213.

land, *n.a-stem*, land 250, 1270.

lang, *adj.*, long 432; lange *adv.*, long 602; *comp.* 576.

lār, *f.ō-stem*, instruction, doctrine 286, 335, 432, 497.

lārsmiþ, *m.a-stem*, scholar 203.

lăst, *m.a-stem*, track; on laste, behind 30.

late, *adv.*, late 708.

lăttēow, *m.wa-stem*, [LATTEW]; lord, leader 1209; lăttīow 520, 898.

lăþ, *adj.*, hateful 30, 94, 142; *superl.* 977.

laðian, *w.v.*(2), [LATHE]; invite 383, 551, 556.

lăðlīc, *adj.*, hateful 520.

(ge)lǣdan, *w.v.*(1), bring 241, 714, 968, 1183.

lǣne, *adj.*, transitory 1270.

lǣran, *w.v.*(1), [LERE]; teach 173, 522, 529, 1205.

lǣs, lǣst, *see* lȳtel.

(ge)lǣstan, *w.v.*(1), [LAST¹]; per-

form, achieve 368, 1165, 1196, 1207.

lǣtan, *v.*(7), cause 237, 250, 818; leort 1104.

lēaf, *n.a-stem*, leaf 1226.

gelēafa, *m.n-stem*, faith 491, 965, 1035, 1136.

gelēafful, 959, gelēaffull, 1047, *adj.*, full of faith.

leahtor, *m.a-stem*, [LAHTER]; sin 838.

leahtorlēas, *adj.*, sinless 1208.

lēan, *n.a-stem*, [LEAN¹]; reward 824.

lēas, *adj.*, [LEASE]; lacking, false 422, 497, 1300.

lēas, *n.a-stem*, [LEASE¹]; lie 576, 580.

lēasung, *f.ō-stem*, lie 689; lēasingum 1122.

lēf, *adj.*, infirm 1213.

lēgen, *adj.*, fiery 756.

leger, *n.a-stem*, [LAIR¹]; resting place 602.

lencten, *m.a-stem*, spring 1226.

lēod, *f.ō-stem*, [LEDE]; *pl.* people 20, 163, 181, 666.

gelēodan, *v.*(2), grow 1226.

lēodfruma, *m.n-stem*, leader 191.

lēodgebyrga, *m.n-stem*, prince 203; leodgebyrgean 556.

lēodhata, *m.n-stem*, tyrant 1300.

lēodhwæt, *adj.*, courageous 11n.

lēodmǣg, *m.a-stem*, compatriot 380.

lēodmægen, *n.a-stem*, host of men 272.

lēof, *adj.*, dear 511, 1035, 1205; *comp.* 606; *superl.* 523.

lēoflīc, *adj.*, lovely 286.

lēofspell, *n.a-stem*, glad tidings 1016.

lēoht, *n.a-stem*, light 7, 298, 486, 733, 947, 1122.

lēoht, *adj.*, light, bright, clear 163, 491, 736, 1115, 1136, 1245n;

lēohte, adv., brightly, gladly 92, 965.

lēoht, adj., light 173.

lēoma, m.n-stem, [LEAM¹]; light gleam, radiance 1294.

leomu, see lim.

leornian, w.v.(2), learn 397.

leornungcræft, m.a-stem, learning 380.

leoðorūn, f.ō-stem, wise counsel ? 522n.

leoðucræft, m.a-stem; art of poetry ?, skill ? 1250n.

lesan, v.(5), [LEASE¹]; gather 1237.

gelettan, w.v.(1), hinder, withstand 94.

līc, n.a-stem, [LICH]; body 877, 882.

gelīc, adj., like 1320.

gelīce, adv., like; superl. geliccost 1271.

līchoma, m.n-stem, [LICHAM]; body 736.

līf, n.a-stem, life 137, 305, 526, 575, 877.

līfdæg, m.a-stem, lifetime 441.

līffruma, m.n-stem, giver of life 335.

līfgan, w.v.(3), live 311, 450, 486.

līfweard, m.a-stem, guardian of life 1035.

līfwynn, f.i-stem, joy in life 1268.

līg, mn.i-stem, [LEYE]; flame 580, 1300.

līgcwalu, f.ō-stem, fiery torment 296.

līge, m.i-stem, lie 307, 575, 666.

līgesearu, n.wa-stem, wile 208.

līgesynnig, adj., deceitful 898.

lim, n.a-stem, limb 882.

gelimpan, v.(3), happen 271, 441, 962, 1154.

limsēoc, adj., maimed 1213.

lindgeborga, m.n-stem, warrior 11n.

lindwered, n.a-stem, troop with shields 142.

lindwīgend, m.cons-stem, warrior 270.

gelīðan, v.(1), [LITHE¹]; depart, complete a journey 249, 1268.

līxan, w.v.(1), shine 23, 1115.

loc, n.a-stem, clasp 1026.

loca, m.n-stem, [LOKE]; imprisonment 181.

lōcian, w.v.(2), look 87.

lof, mn.a-stem, [LOF]; praise 212, 747.

lofian, w.v.(2), [LOVE²]; praise 453.

lūcan, v.(2), [LOUK¹]; set a jewel 264.

lufe, f.n-stem, love 491.

lufian, w.v.(2), love 597.

lufu, f.ō-stem, love 936.

lungre, adv., forthwith 30.

lust, m.ua-stem, pleasure 138, 702.

gelȳfan, w.v.(1), believe 518, 795.

lyft, mfn.i-stem, [LIFT¹]; sky, air 733, 1270.

lyftlācende, adj., moving hither and thither in the air 795.

lȳsan, w.v.(1), [LEESE²]; redeem 296.

lȳt, adv., [LITE⁴]; few 63.

lȳtel, adj., little 272, 959; comp. 48; lȳtle, adv., a little 664.

lȳthwōn, adv., few 142.

M

mā, see miclum

magan, pret.pres.(5), be able 33, 160, 166, 448, 511, 581, 632, 677, 978, 1158, 1177n, 1291.

man, m.cons-stem, man 16, 326, 660, 871; indef.pron., one 358.

mān, n.a-stem, [MAN²]; evil 626, 1296, 1317.

mānfrēa, m.n-stem, wicked ruler 941.

mānfremmende, adj., sinful 906.

102

gemang, *n.a-stem*, crowd; on...
gemang, among 96.

manig, *adj.pron.*, many 231, 969,
1016; monige 499; manegum
15.

manrīm, *mn.a-stem*, number of
men 650.

mānþēāw, *m.wa-stem*, sinful
custom 929.

mānweorc, *adj.*, sinful 811.

maþelian, *w.v.*(2), [MATHELE];
speak 332.

māðum, *m.a-stem*, treasure 1258.

mǣg, *m.a-stem*, [MAY¹]; kins-
woman 330.

mǣgen, *n.a-stem*, strength, host
55, 347, 1222; mǣgn 408.

mǣgencyning, *m.a-stem*, mighty
king 1247.

mǣgenþrym, *m.i-stem*, majesty
734.

mǣgn, see mǣgen.

mǣl, *n.a-stem*, [MEAL¹]; season
986.

mǣlan, *w.v.*(1), [MELE]; speak
351, 537.

mǣre, *adj.*, [MERE¹]; famous,
glorious 214, 340, 863, 969, 989,
1063, 1222; *superl.* 1012.

mǣrðu, *f.ō-stem*, glory 15.

mearcpæþ, *m.a-stem*, road
through border territory 233.

mearh, *m.a-stem*, horse 55, 1175.

medoheal, *f.ō-stem*, meadhall
1258.

melda, *m.n-stem*, [cp MELD V.¹];
informer 428.

(ge)mengan, *w.v.*(1), [MENG];
mingle, compound 306, 1296.

menigo, 870, mengo, 377,
mengu, 225; *f.ō-*stem, crowd,
multitude.

mennisc, *adj.*, human 6.

meotod, *m.a-stem*, creator, God
366; meotudes 461; metudes
1318.

merestrǣt, *f.ō-stem*, [MERE¹ +];
sea-road 242.

metan, *v.*(5), measure 1262.

(ge)mētan, *w.v.*(1), [YMETE];
meet, find 116, 832, 870,
985.

metelēās, *adj.*, without food
612.

gemetgian, *w.v.*(2), [cp METE¹];
moderate 1293.

metud, see meotod.

mēðe, *adj.*, weary, miserable 612,
811.

meðel, *n.a-stem*, council 546.

meðelhēgende, *adj.*, deliberating 279n.

meðelstede, *m.i-stem*, meeting
place 554.

miclum, 875 myclum, 839,
adv., much; *comp.* mā, [MO];
more 434.

mid, *prep. w.acc.*, with 275; *w.dat.*,
amongst 328; at 105; *w.instr.*,
by means of 92.

middangeard, *m.a-stem*, [MID-
DENERD]; world 6, 809.

middel, *m.a-stem*, middle 863,
1296.

mīdl, *n.a-stem*, bit 1175.

miht, *f.i-stem*, might 15, 295, 337,
584.

mihtig, *adj.*, mighty 680, 941.

milde, *adj.*, gracious 1042.

mīlpæþ, *m.a-stem*, road with mile-
stones ? 1262.

milts, *f.jō-stem*, [MILCE]; mercy
501.

mīn, *adj.*, my, mine 163, 349, 436,
438, 447, 535, 656, 816, 906, 917,
929.

mīðan, *v.*(1), [MITHE]; conceal
28.

mōd, *n.a-stem*, mind, heart, spirit
268, 377n, 554, 597.

mōdblind, *adj.*, spiritually blind
306.

mōdcræft, *m.a-stem*, intelligence 408.

mōdgemynd, *fn.i-stem*, mind, intelligence 381, 839.

mōdgeþanc, *m.a-stem*, opinion 535.

mōdig, *adj.*, proud 138, 1192, 1262.

mōdor, *f.r-stem*, mother 214, 340.

mōdsefa, *m.n-stem*, mind 875.

mōdsorg, *f.o-stem*, sorrow 61.

molde, *f.n-stem*, [MOULD¹]; earth 55.

moldweg, *m.a-stem*, earth 467.

mōnaþ, *m.cons-stem*, month *1228*n.

monig, *see* manig.

monigfeald, *adj.*, manifold 644.

morgenspel, *n.a-stem*, news brought in the morning 969.

mōrland, *n.a-stem*, wilderness 612.

morðor, *mn.a-stem*, sin, crime 428.

morðorhof, *n.a-stem*, place of torment 1303.

morðorsleht, *m.i-stem*, [SLEIGHT²]; slaughter 650.

gemōt, *n.a-stem*, meeting 279.

mōtan, *pret.pres.*(6), be possible 175, 433, 905, 915, 1004.

mund, *f.ō-stem*, hand 729.

mūþ, *m.a-stem*, mouth 660.

mycel, *adj.*, much, large 44, 426, 597, 646n, 734; *superl.* 31, 35, 274, 381, 983.

gemyltan, *w.v.*(*1*), melt 1312.

gemynd, *fn.i-stem*, memory, mind 1232, 1247.

gemynde, *adj.*, mindful 1063.

myndgian, *w.v.*(*2*), remember 657.

gemyndig, *adj.*, mindful 213n, 266, 818.

myngian, *w.v.*(*2*), [MING]; admonish 1078.

N

nāhton, *see* āgan.

nales, 359, nālles, 817, *adv.*, by no means.

nama, *m.n-stem*, name 78, 418, 465.

nāt, *see* witan.

nāthwylc, *pron.*, someone 73.

nǣfre, *adv.*, never 388.

nægel, *m.a-stem*, nail 1064, 1077, 1108, 1157; nǣglan, 1127.

nǣnig, *pron.*, none 505.

nǣre, nǣron, nǣs, *see* wǣs.

nǣs, *m.a-stem*, abyss, pit 831.

ně, *neg.adv.*, not, nor 28, 221, 572.

nēah, *adv.*, nigh 66.

geneahhe, *adv.*, frequently 1064.

nēan, *adv.*, clearly, close at hand 657.

nearo, *f.wō-stem*, imprisonment, difficulty 711, 1102.

nearolīc, *adj.*, grievous 912.

nearusearu, *n.wa-stem*, evil, cunning 1108.

nearusorg, *f.ō-stem*, affliction 1260.

nearwe, *adv.*, closely 1157.

nēat, *n.a-stem*, ox 357.

nēawest, *f.i-stem*, neighbourhood 67.

nēdcleofa, *see* nȳdcleofa.

(ge)nēgan, *w.v.*(*1*), address 287, 385.

(ge)nemnan, *w.v.*(*1*), [NEMN]; call, tell of 78, 740, 1194.

nēol, *adj.*, deep 831.

nēolnes, *f.jō-stem*, abyss 942.

neorxnawang, *m.a-stem*, Paradise 755.

nēosan, *w.v.*(*1*), visit 152.

neoðan, *adv.*, [NETHEN]; from below 1114.

nēowe, *see* nīwe.

generian, *w.v.*(*1*), save 132, 163.

nerigend, *m.cons-stem*, saviour

1077; **nergend** 461, **nergendes** 465.

nesan, *v.*(5), survive 1003n.

nigoða, *num.adj.*, ninth 869, 873.

niht, *f.cons-stem*, night 198, 483, 694, 1227.

nihthelm, *m.a-stem*, cover of night 78.

nihtlang, *adj.*, nightlong 67.

(ge)niman, *v.*(4), [NIM]; take 447, 599, 676, 1279.

nis, *see* **beon**.

niþ, *m.a-stem*, [NITH(E)]; enmity 837, 912.

niðas, *m.ja-stem pl.*, men 465.

niðer 831, **nyðer** 942, *adv.*, below.

nioheard, *adj.*, bold 195.

geniola, *m.n-stem*, enmity, torment 701.

niwe, *adj.*, new 195, 1102; **neowne** 869; **niwan stefne**, afresh 1060.

niwigan, *w.v.*(2), renew 940.

no, *adv.*, [NO¹]; never 779.

noldon, *see* **willan**.

nu, *adv.*, now 313; *conj.*, since, now that 534, 635.

nuða, *adv.*, [NOWTHE]; just now 539.

nydcleofa, *m.n-stem*, [+ CLEVE²]; prison 711; **nedcleofan** 1275.

nydgefera, *m.n-stem*, inevitable companion 1260n.

nydþearf, *f.o-stem*, necessity 657.

nysse, nyste *see* **witan**.

nyton, *see* **witan**.

nyðer, *see* **niðer**.

O

of, *prep.w.dat.*, of, from 75, 181, 186.

ofen, *m.a-stem*, furnace 1311.

ofer, *prep.w.acc.*, over 31; after 432; in spite of 372; *w.dat.*, upon 732.

ofermægen, *n.a-stem*, superior strength 64.

oferswiðan, *w.v.*(1), overcome 93, 957n, 1177.

oferþearf, *f.o-stem*, great need 521n.

oferwealdend, *m.cons-stem*, lord 1235.

ofost, *f.i-stem*, haste 44.

ofstlice, *adv.*, quickly 225.

oft, *adv.*, often 238.

on, *prep.w.acc.*, on 347; in 654; into 108; for 223; onto 717; *w.dat.*, in 28; on 37; at 59; among 753; **on...gemang**, *see* **gemang**; **on...weard**, *see* **weard**.

onælan, *w.v.*(1), [ANNEAL]; burn 950.

onbindan, *v.*(3), unbind 1249.

onbregdan, *v.*(3), start up 75.

onbrydan, *w.v.*(1), inspire 1094; **inbryrded** 841.

oncer, *m.a-stem*, anchor 252.

oncnawan, *v.*(7), recognize 362, 965.

oncweðan, *v.*(5), answer 324, 573.

oncyrran, *w.v.*(1), change 503, 610.

oncyðig, *adj.*, revealing 724n.

ond, *conj.*, and 2, 15, 20.

ondrædan, *v.*(7), dread 81.

onfon, *v.*(7), [ONFANG]; receive 192, 335.

ongean, 43, **ongen**, 609, *prep.w. dat.*, against, with.

onginnan, *v.*(3), begin 157, 303.

ongitan, *v.*(5), [ANGET]; understand, recognize 288, 359, 464.

onhyldan, *w.v.*(1), [+ HIELD]; bow 1098.

onhyrdan, *w.v.*(1), strengthen 840.

onleon, *v.*(1), bestow 1245.

onlice, *adv.* [ANLIKE *a.*]; similarly 99.

onlūcan, v.(2), [UNLOUK]; unlock 1250.

onmēdla, m.n-stem, pomp 1265.

onscunian, w.v.(2), reject 370.

onsendan, w.v.(1), send, yield up 120, 480, 1088.

onsīon, see onsȳn.

onsponnan, v.(7), open 86n.

onsȳn, f.i-stem, [ONSENE]; face 745; onsīon 349.

ontȳnan, w.v.(1), [UNTINE]; disclose 1229, 1248.

onwindan, v.(3), open 1249.

onwrēon, v.(1), [UNWRY]; disclose, manifest 589, 1071, 1123, 1242; inwrīge 812.

open, adj., open 647.

geopenian, w.v.(2), open, reveal 791, 1230; geopenigean 1101.

orcnǣwe, adj., evident 229.

ord, m.a-stem, point, spear, beginning, best of a class 140, 235, 393, 590n, 1186; æfter orde, from the beginning 1154.

*orscylde, adj., guiltless 423n.

oþ, prep.w.acc., [oþ] until 139.

ōðer, adj.pron., other 233, 506, 540.

ōðfæstan, w.v.(1), inflict 477.

ōððæt, conj., until 865.

ōððe, conj., or 74.

ōðȳwan, see ætywan.

ōwiht, pron., anything 571.

P

plegean, w.v.(2), move quickly, clap the hands 245, 805n.

R

rād, f.ō-stem, journey 981.

rador, see rodor.

radorcyning, see rodercining.

rand, m.a-stem, shield 50.

raþe, see hraðe.

rǣd, m.a-stem, counsel, wisdom, authority 156, 553, 918, 1008.

rǣdan, v.(7), advise; reord 1022.

gerǣde, n.ja-stem, [cp IREDE a]; equipage, agency ?, 1053n.

rǣdgeþeaht, fn.i-stem, counsel 1051.

rǣdþeahtende, pres.part., wise, deliberating 449.

rǣran, w.v.(1), raise 443, 953.

rēc, m.i-stem, smoke 794, 803.

(ge)reccan, w.v.(1), [RECCHE]; expound 281, 553, 649.

*reodian, w.v.(2), sift 1238n.

rēonig, adj., sorrowful, 1082; rēonian 833.

rēonigmōd, adj., gloomy-hearted 320.

reordberend, m.cons-stem, human being 1282.

reordian, w.v.(2), [RERD(E)]; speak 405.

rēotan, v.(2), lament 1082.

gerestan, w.v.(1), cease 1082.

rīce, n.ja-stem, [RICHE]; kingdom 13, 40, 59.

rīce, adj., powerful 411; superl. 1234.

ricene, adv., quickly 607.

rīcsian, w.v.(2), [cp RIXLE]; rule 434, 773.

rīdan, v.(1), ride 50.

riht, n.a-stem, right, law, truth, judgement 372, 879, 909, 1282; ryhte 369.

riht, adj., true, right 13, 281; rihte, adv., rightly 553; ryhte 1074.

rīm, mn.a-stem, [RIME²]; number 2n, 284, 635.

rīmtalu, f.ō-stem, number 819.

rinc, m.a-stem, [RINK¹]; warrior 46.

rōd, f.ō-stem, cross 103, 147, 219, 482, 833, 879.

rodercining, *m.a-stem*, king of heaven *1074*n; radorcyninges 624; rodorcyninges 886.

rodor, *m.a-stem*, firmament 206, 855; roderum, rodera 13, 482; radores 794.

rōf, *adj.*, renowned 50.

gerūm, *n.a-stem*, space; on gerūm, away 320n.

rūm, *adj.*, spacious; *comp.* 1240.

rūn, *f.ō-stem*, [ROUN]; secret, mystery, rune, counsel 333, 411, 1261.

ryht(e), *see* riht(e).

gerȳman, *w.v.(1)*, [+ RIME⁴]; extend 1248.

ryne, *m.i-stem*, [RUNE¹]; orbit 794.

gerȳne, *n.ja-stem*, [cp ROUN]; secret, mystery 280, 566.

S

sācerdhād, *m.a-stem*, priesthood 1054.

sacu, *f.ō-stem*, [SAKE]; strife 905, 940, 1030.

salor, *n.cons-stem*, [cp SALE¹]; hall 382.

same, some, *adv.*, *see* swa.

(ge)samnian, *w.v.(2)*, [SAM¹, SOMNE¹]; assemble, collect 19, 26, 55.

samod, 728, somed, 95, *adv.*, [SAMED]; together.

sanctus, saint 504.

sand, *n.a-stem*, sand 251n.

sang, *m.a-stem*, song 29.

sār, *n.a-stem*, wound, pain 479, 697, 940.

sāwl, *f.ō-stem*, soul 461, 889, 905, 1171.

sāwllēas, *adj.*, dead 876.

sæ, *mf.i-stem*, sea 240, 728.

sæcc, *f.jō-stem*, strife 1177.

sæcg, *see* secg.

sæfearoþ, *m.a-stem*, sea-shore 251.

sæl, *mf.i-stem*, [SELE]; joy 194.

sælan, *w.v.(1)*, [SEAL²]; moor 228.

gesælig, *adj.*, [ISELI]; blessed 955.

sæmearh, *m.a-stem*, ship 228, 245.

sæne, *adj.*, reluctant 220.

sceacan, *v.(6)*, [SHAKE]; hasten away 633.

(ge)scēadan, *v.(7)*, [SHED]; decide, rule over(?) 149, 709.

gesceaft, *mn.a-f.i-stem*, [SHAFT¹]; creature, creation, object 183, 728, 893.

scealc, *m.a-stem*, [SHALK]; servant 692.

sceamu, *f.ō-stem*, shame 470.

gesceap, *n.a-stem*, [SHAPE]; created thing, object 789.

scēat, *m.a-stem*, [SHEET¹]; corner, place of concealment 583.

sceaða, *m.n-stem*, [SCATHE]; wretch 761, 956.

scēawian, *w.v.(2)*, appear, look at 58n, 345n.

sceolu, *f.ō-stem*, [SHOAL²]; band 762.

sceððan, *v.(6)*, [cp SCATHE]; harm 310.

scīnan, *w.v.(1)*, shine 742, 1114.

scippend, 370, scyppend, 790, *m.cons-stem*, [SHEPPEND]; creator.

scīr, *adj.*, [SHIRE]; bright, radiant 310, 370.

scirian, *w.v.(1)*, assign 1231.

gescrīfan, *v.(1)*, [+ SHRIVE]; decree 1046.

scrīðan, *v.(1)*, glide 237.

scūfan, *v.(2)*, push 692.

sculan, *pret.pres.(4)*, be obliged to, be necessary 210, 367, 545, 673, 763, 837, 895.

scūr, *m.a-stem*, shower 117.

scyld, *f.i-stem*, guilt 470.

scyldful, *adj.*, sinful 310.

scyldig, *adj.*, [SHILDY]; guilty 692.

scyldwyrcende, *pres.part.*, sinful 761.

scyndan, *w.v.*(*1*), hasten 30.

gescyrdan, *w.v.*(*1*), destroy 141n.,

scyppend, *see* **scippend**.

sē, sēo, þæt, *1. pron. adj.art.*, the, that; *sg.* 11, 39, 70, 86, 93, 94, 98, 100, 185, 243, 324, 610, 925n; **sīo** 254; **sēo** 266; **þane** 294; **to þæs**, to such an extent 704; **þæs þe**, from the time when 4; **þæs**, on this account, concerning this 157, 210; **þæs þe**, because 956; **þē, þȳ**, the *with comp.* 96, 795; **to þan**, to such an extent 703; *pl.* 153, 169, 277, 285, 357, 431, 450, 652; **þan** 1127. *2. rel. pron.*, who, which, he, she, those who, that which 101, 172, 191, 243, 398, 423, 568, 570, 709, 739n, 826, 1195n, 1201. *3. combined with the relative particle* 154, 303, 508, 896, 974, 1161; **þæs...þe** 298.

searocræft, *m.a-stem*, cunning 1025.

searoþanc, *m.a-stem*, wisdom 414; **searuþancum** 1189.

sēaþ, *m.ua-stem*, [SEATH]; pit 693.

(ge)sēcean, *w.v.*(*1*), [ISECHE]; seek, enquire, visit 216, 230, 255, 319, 322, 325, 1179, 1280; secean 1148.

secg, *m.ja-stem*, [SEGGE[1]]; man 47, 97, 552; **sæcg** *1256m*; **secggas** 260.

(ge)secgan, *w.v.*(*3*), [ISEGGEN]; say, speak 190, 366, 623, 665, 674, 856, 984; **secggan** 160; **gesecggan** 168.

sefa, *m.n-stem*, mind, heart 173, 376, 382.

gesēfte, *adj.*, easy to bear, *superl.* 1295.

segn, *mn.a-stem*, [SEINE[2]]; banner 124.

sēlest, *see* **gōd; sēl, sēlost**, *see* **wel**.

self, *see* **sylf**.

sellan, *w.v.*(*1*), give 182, 527; **gesyllan** 1284.

semninga, *adv.*, suddenly 1109.

sendan, *w.v.*(*1*), send 457, 930, 1199.

seofeða, *num.adj.*, seventh 697.

seofon, *num.*, seven 694.

seolf, *see* **sylf**.

seolfren, *adj.*, [SILVERN]; silver 1025.

gesēon, *v.*(*5*), [ISEE]; see 88, 1120, 1308; **geseh** 841; **gesǣgon** 68; **gesāwon** 1110; **gesīon** 243.

seonoþdōm, *m.a-stem*, assembly's decree 552.

sēpan, *w.v.*(*1*), instruct 530.

seraphin, seraphim 754.

(ge)settan, *w.v.*(*1*), place, establish, accomplish, beset 479, 495, 654, 658, 738, 1004, 1054, 1135.

gesēðan, *w.v.*(*1*), prove 581.

sīd, *adj.*, [SIDE]; broad, extensive, capacious 158, 376, 728, 1289; **sīde**, *adv.*, widely; **sīde ond wīde**, far and wide 277.

sīdweg, *m.a-stem*, distant land 282.

sige, *m.i-stem*, [SIƷE]; victory 144.

sigebēacen, *n.a-stem*, sign of victory 168, 887, 974.

sigebēam, *m.a-stem*, tree of victory 420, 846, 964, 1027.

sigebearn, *n.a-stem*, victorious son 481.

sigecwēn, *f.i-stem*, victorious queen 260.

sigelēan, *n.a-stem*, reward for victory 527.

sigelēoþ, *n.a-stem*, [+ LEOTH]; victory cry 124n.

sigeróf, *adj.*, triumphant 47, 71, 158.

sigespéd, *f.i-stem*, victory 1171.

sigor, *m.os-a-stem*. victory 85, 346, *1180*n, 1182.

sigorbéacen, *n.a-stem*, sign of victory 984.

sigorcynn, *n.ja-stem*, victorious race 754.

sigorléan, *n.a-stem*, reward of victory 623.

gesihþ, *f.ō-stem*, sight 614; **gesyhþ** 98; **gesyhðe** 184n.

sinc, *n.a-stem*, treasure 194.

sincgim, *m.a-stem*, jewel 264.

sincweorðung, *f.ō-stem*, costly gift 1218.

sindréam, *m.a-stem*, eternal joy 740.

singál, *adj.*, perpetual 905.

singállīce, *adv.*, perpetually 746.

singan, *v.(3)*, sing 109, 337, 746, 1153.

siomian, *w.v.(2)*, abide 694.

(ge)sīon, *see* **(ge)sēon**.

sionoþ, *m.a-stem*, assembly 154.

sioððan, *see* **sioððan**.

(ge)sittan, *v.(5)*, sit 731, 867.

sīþ, *m.a-stem*, [SITHE¹]; journey, experience, time 111, 247, 817, 910, 1000.

sīþ, *adv.*, late 74.

sīðdæg, *m.a-stem*, later time 639.

sīðfæt, *mn.a-stem*, journey 220, 229.

sīðian, *w.v.(2)*, [SITHE¹]; journey 95.

sīððan, *adv.*, [SITHEN]; afterwards, since 271, 636; **sioððan**, 1146; *conj.*, when 230; **syððan**, from the time when 116; **syð-ðan**, from the time when 116; **syððan furðum**, *see* **furðum**.

slǣp, *m.a-stem*, sleep 69.

slīðe, *adj.*, cruel 856.

smǣte, *adj..* [SMEAT]; refined 1309.

sméagan, *w.v.(2)*, consider 413.

snottor, *adj.*, [SNOTER]; wise 1189; *superl.* **snoterestum** 277.

snūde, *adv.*, quickly 154.

snyrgan, *w.v.(1)*, hasten 244.

snyttro, *f.ō-stem*, wisdom 154, 293.

some, *see* **same**.

somed, *see* **samod**.

sōna, *adv.*, forthwith 47, 85, 222.

sorg, *f.ō-stem*, sorrow 694, 921, 1030.

sorgian, *w.v.(2)*, sorrow 1081.

sorgléas, *adj.*, joyful; *comp.* 97.

sōþ, *n.a-stem*, truth 307, 395; **tō sōðe**, of a truth 160.

sōþ, *adj.*, true 461, 777, 887, 891.

sōðcwide, *m.i-stem*, true saying 530.

sōðcyning, *m.a-stem*, true king 444.

sōðfæst, *adj.*, pious 7, 1289.

sōðfæstnes, *f.jō-stem*, faith, piety 1148.

sōðlīce, *adv.*, truly 200.

sōðwundor, *n.a-stem*, true wonder 1121.

spāld, *n.a-stem*, [SPOLD]; spittle 300.

spéd, *f.i-stem*, success, abundance 366, 1181.

spéowan, *w.v.(1)*, spew 297.

spild, *m.cons-stem*, destruction 1118.

gespon, *n.a-stem*, [cp SPAN²]; clasp, link 1134n.

spōwan, *v.(7)*, succeed 916.

(ge)sprecan, *v.(5)*, speak 332, 667, 1285.

stærcedfyrhþ, *adj.*, resolute 38.

stæþ, *n.a-stem*, [STAITHE]; bank, shore 38, 60.

stān, *m.a-stem*, stone 492, 565, 613, 615.

stănclif, *n.a-stem*, rock, cliff 135.

standan, *v.(6)*, stand, rise 113, 227, 232, 577.

stăngefōg, *n.a-stem*, mason's art 1020.

stăngripe, *m.i-stem, see* **worpian.**

stănhlĭp, *n.a-stem*, [+ LITH¹]; cliff; **stanhlĕŏŏum,** 653.

staŏelian, *w.v.(2)*, [STATHEL]; make firm, establish 427, 796; **staŏolian,** 1093.

stæppan, *v.(6)*, advance, move 121.

gesteald, *n.a-stem*, dwelling 801.

stĕām, *m.a-stem*, steam, vapour 802.

stearc, *adj.*, [STARK]; hard, obstinate 565, 615n.

stede, *m.i-stem*, place 135.

stedewang, *m.a-stem*, place 675.

stefn, *f.ō-stem*, [STEVEN¹]; voice 747.

stefn, [STEVEN²]; *see* **nīwe.**

stĕnan, *see* 151n.

stĭŏhycgende, *pres.part.*, [STITH +]; bold, 683, 716.

stĭŏhīdīg, *adj.*, resolute 121.

stŏw, *f.wō-stem*, place 653, 675, 683, 716.

strang, *adj.*, strong 703.

strĕām, *m.a-stem*, stream 1200.

strūdan, *v.(2)*, rob 904.

stunde, *adv.*, [cp STOUND sb.¹]; forthwith 723.

stundum, *adv.*, [STUNDUM]; at times 121.

sum, *pron. adj.*, a certain one 131, 132, 479.

sumer, *m.ua-stem*, summer 1227.

sund, *n.a-stem*, [SOUND¹]; sea 228.

gesund, *adj.*, safe 996.

sundor, *adv.*, apart 407.

sundorwīs, *adj.*, singularly wise 588.

sunne, *f.n-stem*, sun 1109.

sunu, *m.u-stem*, son 222, 447, 474, 1199.

sūsl, *n.a-f.ō-stem*, torture 771, 943, 949.

swā, *adv.*, so, thus 163, 271; such 541; like, as 1309; **swā some, same,** likewise 653, 1206; *conj.*, when, as, as soon as 87, 100; as far as 971; **swā…swā þĕāh,** although…yet 498–500; **swā …swā,** either…or 325; *rel.* who 190; **swā þæs,** whose 340.

swæs, *adj.*, dear 447.

swāmian, *w.v.(2)*, grow dark 629n.

sweart, *adj.*, [SWART]; black; *superl.* 930.

swefan, *v.(5)*, [SWEVE]; sleep 70.

swefen, *n.a-stem*, dream 71.

swegl, *n.a-stem*, heaven 75, 507.

***swelling,** *f.ō-stem*, swelling sail 245n.

sweng, *m.i-stem*, blow 239.

gesweorcan, *v.(3)*, [SWERK]; darken 855.

sweord, *n.a-stem*, sword 756.

sweordgeniŏla, *m.n-stem*, enemy 1180.

swĕŏt, *n.a-stem*, troop 124n.

sweotole, *adv.*, [cp SUTEL *a.*]; clearly 26.

sweotollīce, *adv.*, clearly 690.

geswerigan, *w.v.(1)*, swear 686.

geswīcan, *v.(1)*, [ISWIKE]; desist 516.

swīge, *adj.*, [cp SWIE v.]; still 1274.

swilt, 677, **swylt,** 447, *m.i-stem*, death.

swinsian, *w.v.(2)*, resound 240.

swiþra, *comp. adj.*, [SWITHER]; right 347.

swīŏe, *adv.*, [SWITH]; greatly 663; *superl.* 668.

geswiŏrian, *w.v.(2)*, [cp SWITHER¹]; diminish 698, 1263.

swonrād, *f.ō-stem,* sea 996.

swylc, *pron.,* such 571; which 32; **swylce,** *adv.,* likewise 3; as it were 1112.

swylt, *see* **swilt.**

syb, *f.jō-stem,* [SIB³]; kindred, tribe, peace 26, 446, 598, 1182.

gesyhþ, *see* **gesihþ.**

sylf, *pron.,* self 69, 200, 222, 303, 1000, 1206, 1295; **seolfe** 1120; **selfre** 1199; **seolfne** 488.

gesyllan, *see* **sellan.**

symle, *adv.,* always 469.

syn, *f.jō-stem,* sin 414, 497, 677, 771.

gesȳne, *adj.,* visible 144, 264.

synful, *adj.,* sinful 1295.

synnig, *adj.,* sinful 955.

synwyrcende, *pres.part.,* sinful 395, 943.

syððan, *see* **siððan.**

syx, *num.,* six 740, 741.

syxta, *num.adj.,* sixth 7.

T

tācen, *n.a-stem,* symbol 85, 164, 171, 184; heroic deed 645n; remarkable event 319; **tācnum,** *adv.,* clearly 853.

getācnian, *w.v.(2),* show forth 753.

(ge)tǣcan, *w.v.(1),* teach, show 601, 631, 1074.

tēar, *m.a-stem,* tear 1133.

(ge)tellan, *w.v.(1),* suppose, count 2n; **talde** 908.

tempel, *n.a-stem,* temple 1009, 1021, 1057.

getengan, *w.v.(1),* apply oneself 200.

getenge, *adj.,* near to 228, 1113.

tēona, *m.n-stem,* [TEEN¹]; vexation 987.

tīd, *f.i-stem,* time, hour 193, 873,

1043; **tīdum,** *adv.,* at times 1248.

til, *adj.,* good 325.

getimbran, *w.v.(1),* [TIMBER]; build 1009.

tīonlēg, *mn.i-stem,* destroying flame 1279.

tīr, *m.a-stem,* glory 164, 753.

tīrēadig, *adj.,* glorious 104, 605.

tō, *prep.w.dat.,* to 32; as 10; of 319; with the inflected infinitive 533, *adv.,* too 63; to 1104.

tōgēnes, *prep.w.dat.,* [TOGAINS]; towards, in reply 167, 536.

tōglīdan, *v.(1),* depart 78, 1268.

tohte, *f.n-stem,* battle 1179.

torht, *n.a-stem,* brightness 1248.

torht, *adj.,* bright; *superl.* 164.

torn, *n.a-stem,* grief 1133.

torngeniðla, *m.n-stem,* bitter foe 568.

tōsomne, *adv.,* [TOSAME]; together 1201.

tōweorpan, *v.(3),* destroy 430.

tōwrecan, *v.(5),* scatter 131.

trāg, *f.ō-stem,* affliction 668.

trāg, *adj.,* evil 325, 954.

tredan, *v.(5),* tread 55, 612.

trēo, *n.wa-stem,* tree 107, 706, 1026, 1251; **trīo** 429; **trēow** 664.

trymman, *w.v.(1),* [TRIM]; confirm, draw up in formation 14, 35n.

getrȳwe, *adj.,* faithful 1034.

turfhaga, *m.n-stem,* [+ HAW¹]; sod 829.

twēgen, *num.,* two 2, 853, 879, 1306.

twēntig, *num.,* twenty 829.

twēo, *m.n-stem,* doubt 171, 668.

tyht, *m.i-stem,* [TIGHT¹]; march, motion 53.

getȳn, *w.v.(1),* teach 1017.

getȳnan, *w.v.(1),* [TINE¹]; enclose 721, 920.

þ

þā, adv., [THO]; then 1, 7, conj., when 389; þā gīna, see gīna.

þaflan, w.v.(2), [THAVE]; consent 608.

þanc, m.a-stem, thanks 810.

geþanc, mn.a-stem, thought 267, 1238; geþonc 1286.

þancian, w.v.(2), thank 961.

þanon, adv., [THENNE]; thence 143.

þǣr, adv., there, then 41, 84; conj., where, if 70, 838, adv., would that 978n.

þæt, conj., so that 15; that 144; in order that 375; because 59n,175.

þe, rel.pron., who, which, where 160, 577, 717n; comp.rel. 1278.

þēah, conj., though 48.

þeaht, f.ō-stem, thought 1241.

geþeaht, fn.i-stem, counsel, knowledge 468, 1240.

þeahtian, w.v.(2), take counsel 547.

þearf, f.ō-stem, [THARF]; need 426.

þearl, adj., severe 704.

þēaw, m.wa-stem, [THEW¹]; custom, pl. morality 1210.

þegn, m.a-stem, thane, servant, retainer 151, 487, 540.

þegnung, f.ō-stem, service 738, 744.

(ge)þencan, w.v.(1), think, consider 296, 313, 549.

þēod, f.ō-stem, [THEDE]; nation 185, 448, 539.

þēodcwēn, f.i-stem, empress 1155.

þēoden, m.a-stem, prince 267, 487.

þēodenbealu, n.wa-stem, terrible evil 403.

þēodscipe, m.i-stem, instruction 1166.

þēosterloca, m.n-stem, tomb 485.

þēostorcofa, m.n-stem,[+ COVE¹]; dark chamber 832.

þēostre, adj., [THESTER]; dark 312.

þēostru, f.ō-stem, [THESTER]; darkness 766; þȳstrum 307.

þēowdōm, m.a-stem, service 201.

þēownēd, f.i-stem, bondage 769.

þerscan, v.(3), [THRASH]; beat 358.

þes, adj.pron., this, 92, 162, 312, 402, 468, 576, 630, 700, 703, 748, 857, 905 (see note to 161), 1172.

þicgan, v.(5), [THIG]; receive 1258.

þīn, adj., thy, thine 510, 597, 666, 726, 738, 766, 769, 772, 928, 1088.

þincan, see þyncan.

þing, n.a-stem, thing, condition 409, 608n.

geþinge, n.ja-stem, fate 253.

þinggemearc, n.a-stem, period of time 3n.

þingian, w.v.(2), speak, intercede 77, 494.

geþōht, mn.a-stem, thought 426.

(ge)þolian, w.v.(2), [THOLE]; endure 769, 1292.

geþonc, see geþanc.

þonne, adv., then 50, 446; conj., when 473; than 74; þone 49; since 1177.

þracu, f.ō-stem, attack 45.

þrǣcheard, adj., brave 123.

þrǣgan, w.v.(1), run 1262.

þrāgum, adv., [cp THROW sb.¹]; at times 1238.

þrēā, f.wō-mn.a-stem, violence 1276.

(ge)þrēagan, w.v.(2), [THREA]; torment 321, 1296.

þrēalīc, adj., terrible 426.

þrēanȳd, f.i-stem, cruel necessity 704; þrēanēdum 883.

þrēat, m.a-stem, [THREAT]; band 51, 546.

geþrēatian, w.v.(2), torment 695.

geþrec, *n.a-stem*, press, tumult 114.

þreodian, *see* **þrydian**.

þridda, *num.adj.*, third 185, 854, 883.

þrīe, *num.*, three 2, 483, 846, 857, 1286.

(ge)þringan, *v.(3)*, [THRING]; press forward, throng 40, 123, 329.

þrīste, *adj.*, [THRISTE]; bold, presumptuous 267, 1286; *adv.*, 409.

þrittig, *num.*, thirty 3.

þroht, *m.a-stem*, affliction 704.

þrohtherd, *adj.*, patient 494.

þrosm, *m.a-stem*, vapour 1298.

(ge)þrōwian, *w.v.(2)*, [THROW²]; suffer 421, 519, 563, 768, 854.

þrydian, *w.v.(2)*, deliberate 549; **þreodude** 1238.

þrym, *m.i-stem*, [THRUM¹]; glory 177, 348, 483, 1089.

þrymcyning, *m.a-stem*, king of glory 494.

þrymlīce, *adv.*, gloriously 780.

þrymsittende, *pres.part*, enthroned in glory 810.

þrȳnes, *f.jō-stem*, trinity 177.

þrȳðbord, *n.a-stem*, mighty shield, ship? 151n.

þū, *pron.*, thou 79, 81, 82, 83, 403, 927.

þūf, *m.a-stem*, banner of plumes 123.

þurfan, *pret.pres.(3)*, [THARF]; need 918, 939, 1103.

þurh, *prep.w.acc.*, through, in, because of; 6, 1236n; **þurg** 289; on account of 400.

þurhdrīfan, *v.(1)*, permeate 707.

þurhgēotan, *v.(2)*, [+ YET]; endue 961.

þurhwadan, *v.(6)*, pierce 1065.

þus, *adv.*, thus 189.

þūsend, *num.*, thousand 285, 326.

þyder, *adv.*, thither 548.

þȳlæs, *conj.*, lest 430.

þyncan, *w.v.(1)*, seem 72, 541, 1164; **þince** 532.

þyslīc, *adj.*, such 540, 546.

þȳstru, *see* **þēostru**.

U

ūhta, *m.n-stem*, [UGHTEN]; dawn 105.

unāsecgendlīc, *adj.*, ineffable 466.

unbrǣce, *adj.*, inviolable *1028n.*

unclǣne, *adj.*, unclean 301.

uncūþ, *adj.*, unknown 1101.

uncȳðig, *adj.*, ignorant ? 960n.

undearninga, *adv.*, plainly 405; **undearnunga** 620.

under, *prep.w.acc.dat.*, under 13, 763.

ungelīce, *adv.*, [UNILICHE]; differently 1307.

unhwīlen, *adj.*, eternal 1231.

unlīfgende,*pres.part.*, lifeless 878.

unlȳtel, *adj.*, great, much 283, 871.

unoferswīðed, *past part.*, invincible 1187.

unriht, *n.a-stem*, wrong 472.

unriht, *adj.*, wrong 1041.

unrīme, *adj.*, numberless 61.

unscyldig, *adj.*, guiltless 496.

unscynde, *adj.*, noble 365, 1200.

unslāw, *adj.*, quick 202.

unsnyttro, *f.ō-stem*, folly 946, 1285.

unsōfte, *adv.*, with difficulty 132.

untrāglīce, *adv.*, honestly 410.

untwēonde, *adj.*, unwavering 797.

unweaxen, *past part.*, young 529.

unwīslīce, *adv.*, foolishly 293.

up, *adv.*, up 87.

uppan, *prep.w.dat.*, upon 885.

uppe, *adv.*, aloft 52.

uprador, *m.a-stem*, firmament 730.

upweard, *adv.*, upward 805.
ûrigfeðera, 29, ûrigfeðra, 111, *adj.*, dewy-feathered.
ûser, *adj.*, our 425.
ût, *adv.*, out 45.
ûðweota, *m.n-stem*, [UÞWITE]; wise man, elder 473.

W

wâ, *adv.*, ill 628.
(ge)wadan, *v.*(6), go 246, 1189.
waldan, *see* wealdan.
waldend, *see* wealdend.
wan, *adj.*, dark 53.
wang, *m.a-stem*, [WONG]; place 684.
wansælig, *adj.*, accursed 977; wonsælige 478.
wangstede, *m.i-stem*, place 793.
wannhâl, *adj.*, infirm 1029.
wædl, *f.ō-stem*, [WÆDLE]; want 617.
wæg, *m.i-stem*, [cp WAW¹]; wave 230.
wægflota, *m.n-stem*, [+FLOTE¹]; ship 246.
wæghengest, *m.a-stem*, ship 236.
gewælan, *w.v.*(1), afflict 1243.
wælfel, *adj.*, fierce 53.
wælhlence, *f.n-stem*, coat-of-mail 24.
wælhrēow, *adj.*, cruel 112.
wælrest, *f.jō-stem*, place of rest on the battle field 723.
wælrûn, *f.ō-stem*, slaughter rune 28.
wæpen, *n.a-stem*, weapon 17, 48, 1188.
wæpenþracu, *f.ō-stem*, battle 106.
wær, *f.ō-stem*, [WARE⁴]; covenant, pledge 80, 822.
wærlîc, *adj.*, cunning 544.
wæs, wære, *p.t.sg.*, was, were 1n, 7, 159, 707, 776, 990; *pl.* were 22, 291.

wæstm, *mn.a-f.ō-stem*, [WASTUM]; increase 341.
wæter, *n.a-stem*, water 39.
wæðan, *w.v.*(1), hunt 1273.
wē, *pron.*, we 364, 397, 399, 400, 533, 637.
wêâdæd, *f.i-stem*, deed bringing sorrow 495.
weald, *m.ua-stem*, forest 28.
geweald, *mn.a-stem*, [IWALD]; power 120, 610.
wealdan, *v.*(7), rule 450, 760; walde 800.
wealdend, *m.cons-stem*, [WALD-END]; ruler 4,391; waldend 731.
weallan, *v.*(7), [WALL¹]; be fervent 937.
weard, *m.a-stem*, guardian 153, 384, 1100.
weard, [-WARD]; *in* on... weard, towards 84.
weardian, *w.v.*(2), maintain, guard 135, 1144.
wearhtræf, *n.a-stem*, [WARY +]; hell 926.
weaxan, *v.*(7), grow 12, 547n, 913.
webbian, *w.v.*(2), contrive 309.
wed, *n.ja-stem*, pledge; wed gesyllan, be responsible for 1284.
wêdan, *w.v.*(1), [WEDE]; rage 1273.
wefan, *v.*(5), weave, contrive 1237.
weg, *m.a-stem*, way 1149.
wegan, *v.*(5), [WEIGH¹]; feel 61.
wel, *adv.*, well; *comp.* sêl 795; *superl.* sêlest 374; sêlost 1157.
wêmend, *m.cons-stem*, one who reveals 879.
wêna, *m.n-stem*, expectation 584.
wênan, *w.v.*(1), expect 62, 478, 668, 1103.
(ge)wendan, *w.v.*(1), change, turn away, depart 348, 440, 617, 978, 1046.

weorc, *n.a-stem,* work 110, 1242, 1318.

weorod, weorud, *see* **werod.**

weorpan, *v.(3),* [WARP]; cast 1304.

(ge)weorðan, *v.(3),* [WORTH¹]; become, be, happen 5, 130, 220, 336, 401, 428, 429, 456, 575, 614n, 632, 643, 922, 960, 975, 1191, 1288.

(ge)weorðian, *w.v.(2),* [WORTH²]; honour 150, 177, 822, 890, 1136, 1221.

weoruld, *see* **woruld.**

wer, *m.a-stem* [WERE¹]; man 22, 72, 236, 287, 304, 508, 784.

wergan, *w.v.(1),* [WARY]; curse 294.

wergðu, *f.ð-stem,* damnation 211, 295, 309.

gewerian, *w.v.(1),* clothe 263.

wērig, *adj.,* weary, wretched 357, 387, 762; *cp Beo. ed. Klaeber 133n.*

werod, *n.a-stem,* [WERED]; host; army 19, 39, 48, 53, 230, **weor(u)da** 223, 1149n; **weorodum** 351; **wereda** 1084.

werodlēst, *f.ō-stem,* lack of troops 63.

werþēōd, *f.ō-stem,* nation 17, 643, 968.

westan, *adv.,* [WESTEN]; from the west 1015.

wēsten, *n.ja-stem,* wilderness 611.

wīc, *n.a-f.ō-stem,* [WICK²]; dwelling-place 1037.

wicg, *n.ja-stem,* [WIDGE]; steed 1195.

wīcian, *w.v.(2),* [WICK¹]; encamp 38, 65.

wīd, *adj.,* wide, far; **wīde** *adv.,* widely 131; **on wīdan fēōre, to wīdan fēōre,** *see* **feorh; wīdan fyrhþ,** *see* **fyrhþ.**

wīf, *n.a-stem,* woman 223, 236, 1131.

wīg, *n.a-stem,* [WI]; warfare 19, 112, 131; **wīgges** 824; **wīgge** 48.

wīga, *m.n-stem,* [WYE¹]; warrior 63, 246, 344.

*wīga, *m.n-stem,* the Holy Spirit ? 937n.

wīgend, *m.cons-stem,* warrior 106; **wīggende** 983.

wīgspēd, *f.i-stem,* success in battle 165.

wīgþracu, *f.ð-stem,* strife 430; **wīgþræce** 658.

wiht, *fn.i-stem,* something 684.

wilfægen, *adj.,* joyful 827.

wilgifa, *see* **willgifa.**

willa, *m.n-stem,* joy, will, desire 267, 681, 772; **Dryhtne to willan,** for the Lord's sake 193; **Criste to willan,** for Christ's sake 678.

willan, *anom.v.,* be willing, intend 40, 219, 394, 420, 469, 566, 574, 608, 621, 1079, 1180.

willgifa, *m.n-stem,* ruler 814, 1111; **wilgifan** 221.

willhrēðig, *adj.,* exultant 1116.

willsīþ, *m.a-stem,* joyful errand 223.

willspell, *n.a-stem,* joyful news 993; **wilspella** 983.

wind, *m.a-stem,* wind 1271.

winemǣg, *m.a-stem,* kinsman 1015.

winter, *mn.ua-stem,* winter, year 4.

wintergerīm, *n.a-stem,* number of years 654.

wīr, *m.a-stem,* wire, filigree work 1134n, 1263.

wīs, *adj.,* wise 592; *superl.* 153, 169, 323.

wīsdōm, *m.a-stem,* wisdom 334, 357, 1242.

wīse, *f.n-stem*, matter 684.

wīsfæst, *adj.*, wise 314.

wist, *f.i-stem* [WIST]; food 617.

wita, *m.n-stem*, [WITE¹]; wise man 544.

witan, *pret.pres.*(*1*), know 401n, 419, 459n, 640, 644, 719, 859, 945, 1239.

wītan, *v.*(*1*), [WITE¹]; accuse 416.

gewītan, *v.*(*1*), [IWITE]; depart 94, 1271, 1277.

wīte, *n.ja-stem*, [WITE²]; torment 180, 520, 764.

wītebrōga, *m.n-stem*, terrible punishment 931.

wītedōm, *m.a-stem*, prophecy 1152.

wītga, *m.n-stem*, [WITIE]; wise man, prophet 289, 561, 592, 1188.

gewitt, *n.ja-stem*, understanding 357, 937.

wiþ, *prep.w.acc.*, towards 822; against 403; *w.gen.*, against 616; *w.dat.*, with 307; to 77; against 18.

wiðercyr *m.i-stem*, [+ CHARE¹]; reversal 925.

wiðerhycgende, *pres.part.*, malevolent 951.

wiðersæc, *n.a-stem*, contradiction 569.

wiðhyccgan, *w.v.*(*3*), scorn 618.

wiðrēotan, *v.*(*2*), oppose 369n.

wiðsacan, *v.*(*6*), [WITHSAKE]; deny, refuse, renounce 390, 617, 663, 766, 932, 1039, 1121.

wiðweorpan, *v.*(*3*), spurn 294.

wlanc, *adj.*, [WLONK]; proud 231.

gewlencan, *w.v.*(*1*), [WLENCH]; adorn 1263.

wlītan, *v.*(*1*), look 385.

wlite, *m.i-stem*, [WLITE]; glory 1319.

wlitescȳne, *adj.*, beautiful 72.

wlitig, *adj.*, [WLITI]; beautiful 77, 165, wliti 89; *superl.* 748.

wolcen, *n.a-stem*, [WELKIN]; cloud 89, 1271.

wom, *mn.a-stem*, [WAM]; sin, stain 583.

wōma, *m.n-stem*, harbinger, revelation, sound of battle 19n, 71.

womful, *adj.*, sinful 760.

womsceaða, *m.n-stem*, sinner 1299.

wonhȳdig, *adj.*, foolish 762.

wonsǣlig, *see* wansǣlig.

wōp, *m.a-stem*, lamentation 1131.

word, *n.a-stem*, word 24n, 221, 314, *338*, 544, 581, 945.

wordcræft, *m.a-stem*, eloquence 592, 1237n.

wordcwide, *m.i-stem*, speech 547.

wordgerȳne, *n.ja-stem*, mystic saying 289.

worn, *m.a-stem*, great number 633.

worpian, *w.v.*(*2*), throw; stānum, stāngreopum worpian, stone 492, 823–4.

woruld, *f.i-stem*, world 508, 1141, *1276*; worlde 993; in woruld weorulda, for ever and ever 452.

woruldgedāl, *n.a-stem*, death 581.

woruldrīce, 456, worldrīce 1048, *n.ja-stem*, earthly kingdom.

woruldstund, *f.ō-stem*, time in the world; æfter woruldstundum, in the world 363.

wōþ, *f.ō-stem*, song 748.

wracu, *f.ō-stem*, [WRAKE¹]; retribution, misery 17, 495.

wrāþ, *adj.*, wroth, hostile 165, 459, 1181.

wrāðe, *adv.*, [WROTHE]; perversely 294.

wraðu, *f.ō-stem*, help, support 84, 1029.

wræcmæcg, *m.ja-stem*, [WRACK¹ +]; outcast, wretch; wræc-mæcggas 387

wrǽtlīce, *adv.*, wondrously; *superl.* 1019.

wrecan, *v.(5)*, press forward 121.

wreccan, *w.v.(1)*, [WRECCHE]; rouse 106.

wrēōn, *(v.1)*, [WRY¹]; conceal 583.

gewrit, *n.a-stem*, writing, Scripture 387, 674, 826.

wrīðan, *v.(1)*, [WRITHE]; weave 24.

wrixlan, *w.v.(1)*, [WRIXLE]; change 758.

wrōht, *m.a-f.ō-stem*, slander 309.

wrōhtstæf, *m.a-stem*, calumny 925.

wuldor, *n.a-stem*, [WULDER]; glory 5, 77, 295, 812, *1134*n.

wuldorcyning, *m.a-stem*, king of glory 291, 1321.

wuldorfæst, *adj.*, glorious 966.

wuldorgeofa, *m.n-stem*, giver of glory 681.

wuldorgifu, *f.ō-stem*, glorious gift 1071.

wulf, *m.a-stem*, wolf 28.

wund, *f.ō-stem*, wound 514.

wundor, *n.a-stem*, miracle 363, 826, 866, 1237.

wundorwyrd, *f.i-stem*, wonderful event 1070.

wundrian, *w.v.(2)*, marvel 958.

(ge)wunigan, *w.v.(2)*, [WON]; dwell, inhabit 624, 723, 820, 949, 1027, 1037.

wylm, *m.i-stem*, [WALM¹]; swell, surging fire 39, 764, 1299.

wyn, *f.i-stem*, joy 788, 1039, 1089.

wynbēam, *m.a-stem*, tree of joy 843.

wynsum, *adj.*, joyful 793.

(ge)wyrcan, *w.v.(1)*, [IWURCHE]; work, construct, perform 104, 470, 513, 726, 826, 1019.

(ge)wyrd, *f.i-stem*, [WEIRD]; Providence, event, fact 80, 541, 647, 812n, 1046.

wyrdan, *w.v.(1)*, [WERDE]; destroy 903.

wyrrest, wyrsa, *see* yfel.

wyrðe, *adj.*, [WURTHE]; precious 291.

Y

yfel, *n.a-stem*, evil 493, 901.

yfel, *adj.*, evil; *comp.*, 1039; *superl.* 931.

yfemest, *superl.adj.*, [UVEMEST]; uppermost 1290.

ylde, *see* ilde.

ymb, *prep.w.acc.*, [UMBE]; around, by 39, 136; concerning 214; after 272.

ymbhwyrft, *m.i-stem*, orb, firmament 730.

ymbsellan, *w.v.(1)*, surround 741.

ymbsittend, *m.cons-stem*, neighbour 33.

yppe, *adj.*, [cp UPPE v.]; known 435.

yrfe, *n.ja-stem*, [ERF¹]; heritage 1320.

yrmðu, *f.ō-stem*, [ERMTH(E)]; misery 952; ermðum 767.

yrre, *adj.*, [IRRE]; angry 573; eorne 685.

ȳþ, *f.jō-stem*, [YTHE]; wave 239.

ȳðhof, *n.a-stem*, ship *252*n.

geȳwan, *w.v.(1)*, reveal 488; gehȳwdest 786; geīewed 102.

INDEX OF PROPER NAMES

Printed and bound by CPI Group (UK) Ltd, Croydon, CR0 4YY

13/04/2025

14656586-0002